HOW TO USE THIS BOOK

GW00802303

Before you begin . . .

Why produce a workbook focusing exclusively on men?

- Because in the majority of churches there are more women than men.
- Because we need to help men respond to Jesus. To do so we need to understand how changes in society are affecting them and influencing how they respond.
- Because we need to develop appropriate models for sharing the Christian faith with the widest possible range of men.
- Because we want to ensure that, within Christian circles, we are not perpetuating unhelpful stereotypes about what it means to be a man.

This workbook is written with the understanding that men and women are equal before God, and that promoting any view or value which sustains sexist attitudes is dishonouring to God. It is my desire to address the issues head on, and I hope I have managed to do this in a way which doesn't fall into either stereotyping men or promoting sexist attitudes. Where I have failed on this matter, I offer an apology. I fully recognize that in contemporary society many of the things that can be said about men equally apply to women, but for the sake of brevity I have not continually pointed this out wherever it would apply in the text.

Much of the work in this book has been directly influenced and inspired by Roy McCloughry's *Men and Masculinity: From power to love*. I recommend it for a much fuller approach to the subject. He argues: 'If the Church is to reach men, as it can and as it must, then it must confront the issue of masculinity.' It is with this in mind that I offer this workbook as an attempt to explore issues of masculinity and evangelism among men.

James Lawrence

How to use this book

MEN The Challenge of Change is designed to be used in a variety of ways:

- for personal study
- as a leadership team
- as resource for existing small groups
- to resource existing men's groups
- to help establish new work among men.

The book contains:

Seven **Chapters** focusing on major issues related to men and masculinity. Each **Chapter** contains:

- An introductory **Overview**
- A page of **Start Here** ideas, suggestions and activities. These are designed for use on a 'pick and mix' basis by church leaders or men's group leaders to help review existing ministry among men, and to assist planning further development.
- A page of **Bible Exploration** designed for use in small groups. The explorations are based on encounters between Jesus and seven very different men. Participants are encouraged to select a 'contact man' from outside the group for whom they will pray.

A final section of five **Going Further** sessions for groups that wish to 'dig deeper' into men's issues. Each **Going Further** session contains:

- An icebreaker **Opening Activity**
- A **Main Focus** for the session
- Suggestions for **Further Activity** including ideas for Bible study, prayer and worship.

CHAPTER 1

MISSING: MEN

He was wiry, forty-ish and casually dressed. Taking the initiative, I introduced myself. No, he hadn't been to this particular church before – but, yes, he had recently started going to church.

He recalled his tough early years free from church influence. With disarming frankness he told me of his successful criminal career – his speciality was breaking and entering premises ranging from millionaires' mansions to the headquarters of multi-national corporations.

Recently he had got to know a Christian. She'd invited him along to a Sunday service. That was when his problems began. He told me: 'As I walked towards that front door, I could almost see a slogan painted up in red letters: "You don't belong here." Crazy – but that's how I felt. Getting inside a church turned out to be the toughest break-in of my career.'

Outsider

What had given my new friend the feeling of being pushed away from church by an invisible 'force field'? His background must have accounted for some of his anxiety. But underlying his fear, I detected an unspoken conviction: real men don't go to church. I'm certain his feeling of being an outsider was intensified by the fact that he was a man.

His situation was simply an extreme example of a perception that's common to legions of men today: 'My mother can go to church. So can my sister, my children, or even my partner. But church is not for me.'

Where are they?

Why do so many men feel this way? What keeps them out of our churches? And for those who do want to come inside, why does getting through the front door demand as much nerve as breaking into a bank vault? Why do women outnumber men in virtually every congregation? In short, where are the men? Discovering the answers to these questions is a vitally important task for any Christian with a responsibility for sharing the gospel.

Telling stories...

The church leaders at Malvern Priory assessed their current activities for men. They found that the social side was well catered for in mixed events. Yet they lacked anything specifically focused for men, despite numerous such activities for women. As a result they have started a men's breakfast meeting three times a year. Response so far has been very good. Local organizer Peter identifies timing as a key to their success. 'Most of the men we're in contact with live pressured lives. Three times a year is often enough for it to feel regular, but not too often for them to feel it's just another pressure.'

How did we lose them?

Let's look back at four broad historical trends that have contributed to the mystery of the missing men.

1. The Age of Reason

Much of our present-day thinking emerged in eighteenth-century Europe with the dawning of the Enlightenment, the so-called Age of Reason. According to its leaders, human progress depended on the pursuit of objectivity and scientific inquiry. They came to believe there was a distinction between the world of facts and the world of faith. They valued science, placing it firmly in the public arena, and down-graded religion, relegating it to the status of private opinion. And since the public world was the exclusive domain of men, matters of faith and spirituality became associated with the private, domestic world – the domain of women.

Men, of course, continued to lead the church. But increasingly women took responsibility in the home for the nurture and transmission of spiritual values.

2. The Industrial Revolution

The first half of the last century saw a huge population shift from the countryside to the rapidly expanding industrial cities. An agricultural, community-based way of life gave way to the demands of mass production. Instead of working beside their families in the fields, men worked long hours away from home in factories, mines or offices: their primary role was to be the material provider. By default, care for spiritual matters was left to women.

3. The World Wars

As this century's two major conflicts recede into history, it's easy to forget the unprecedented scale of their casualties. Listening to a radio programme commemorating the eightieth anniversary of the Battle of the Somme, I was horrified to learn that 20,000 men died – not in the whole battle – but on its first day. Countless families lost fathers. The survivors of both world wars emerged with physical, emotional and spiritual scars – and it's understandable that significant numbers of them subsequently 'died' to God, their faith abandoned in the brutality of battle. A veteran told me recently: 'You just don't know what it was like.' His aggressive attitude towards God was a direct result of his wartime experiences.

4. The minister's role

Until relatively recently, the majority of women worked in the home. Most men worked away from home. Women had more opportunity than men to interact with the vicar, minister or other church leaders. Women, too, tended to be more willing than men to talk about personal needs. It's not surprising, therefore, that many men have come to perceive the caring, nurturing aspects of a minister's work as being essentially feminine in character. The fact that ministers' training focuses on pastoral concerns has possibly made many church leaders more proficient at dealing with women than with men.

Unconnected

Many men aged over forty-five have probably had some contact with the church. If the connection has been a positive one, it may have left them with a degree of respect for the church; for them, attending a traditional service will not necessarily be an alienating experience.

But for many men aged under forty-five, church is likely to be much more of a foreign environment. Unfortunately, many Christians have forgotten what it feels like to be an 'outsider' walking into a church for the very first time. The features which make an environment familiar to its regular inhabitants, may be deeply threatening to the newcomer.

Odd men out

A recent experience of being completely out of my depth, renewed my sympathy for people who find themselves in similar, red-faced situations.

I had never been to the dogs before. Arriving at the track in the rural depths of Norfolk, I noticed I was dressed differently from everyone else. No one had warned me that there was a dress code. In return for my entrance fee,

I was handed a book. Unable to make any sense of its contents, I turned to my companion for explanation. Patiently, he introduced me to the mysteries of 'form': the ancestry, training and track records of the animals competing that night. Further study had to wait while he led me to one of many small groups of race-goers. He introduced me to his friends. They nodded hello and continued with their discussion of a subject about which I knew nothing, in language that I couldn't understand. A bell rang and people crowded around a man standing on a box. Amidst a volley of shouting, he chalked hieroglyphics on a blackboard as money changed hands. Then another bell rang and the first race began. This bit I did understand. The first dog across the line was the winner!

On the journey home, I reflected on my experience. Although a grown man, I'd felt lonely, ignorant, vulnerable and unsure of myself.

I began to think about the parallel experience of John, a friend whom I'd invited to church a few weeks before. John is a truck driver and church-going did not feature in his upbringing. What follows is a summary of his first impressions of my 'home turf'.

Telling stories...

The Stable, a community-based church in north London, runs a programme of cabaret evenings. They transform their meeting place into a restaurant, and encourage church members to book a table and bring along friends. Eamon had attended a number of such evenings and confided to his wife (a Christian) that he was fed up with having to talk about Christianity with the people sharing his table. His wife telephoned the minister and asked if there was anything that could be done. At the next cabaret evening they were delighted to find a table for two had been set aside for them. 'Since then Eamon has been so much warmer towards us,' said the minister. 'Flexibility is important to us: it's important to start where men are rather than expecting them to start where we are.'

'First thing I notice is I'm dressed differently from everyone else. I go through the door and someone hands me some books – a small library in fact. Inside people are sitting around chatting. No one goes out of their way to make me feel welcome. The service starts. We're told to turn to page 119. So I look in the middle of the book – common sense. How was I to know that in this book page 119 is at the beginning? Later on there's a strange part when everyone goes down to the front to eat some bread and drink out of a cup. What's going on? Should I join in? Finally there's a bit I understand. When the guy in the funny gear leaves, it means that it's over – and I'm glad!'

Models of evangelism

Even when churches are concerned about the lack of men, the action they take can cause further problems.

Men taking responsibility If women outnumber men in most churches, it seems sensible to encourage them to reach out to partners, sons, fathers and fiancés. But this strategy can pressurize relationships, particularly partnerships. It places an unfair amount of responsibility on women, while at the same time letting the men of the church 'off the hook'.

Beyond the pub In recent years many of the popular strategies for reaching men have promoted activities focused on the pub and on sport. These approaches have aimed to counter the negative image of the 'weak' Christian man. Linked to them has been a concern to reach working-class men, a group noticeably absent from many churches. But while such work deserves to be encouraged, the 'pubs and clubs' approach is not the whole solution. For this reason it's important to think beyond our current 'models of evangelism'. We need to identify and understand what is happening among men today, so that we can develop strategies for reaching the broadest possible range of them.

As others see us

Seeing ourselves as others see us is a painful, but necessary, experience. How would the following three very basic aspects of church life emerge from scrutiny by a first-time male visitor?

- *Arriving at church* 'All the posters on the notice boards were for women's activities. There was nothing for men.'

- *The service* 'I took one look at the clergyman dressed in cassock and surplice and thought, you can't be serious'; 'I was expected to join in action songs – it was like being back in the Cubs'; 'There were so many women and children, I felt like a fish out of water'; 'Some of the songs suggest you're having an affair with Jesus.'

- *The teaching* 'The preacher didn't have much of a clue about the world of work'; 'They're great on theology and abstract concepts – but what about the pressures of life on the building site / stock market / dole queue?' 'All the youth and children's leaders are women – my boys need some male role models.'

Ideas for assessing your current situation

1. Head count Over four or five Sundays ask your church wardens, elders or welcome team to provide a breakdown of church attendance. What is the overall ratio of men to women? Are some services more popular with men? Are there any particular age bands where you have few men but regular women worshippers?

2. Check the children What is the ratio of men to women among your youth and children's workers? Does the ratio vary according to the age group of the children or young people? Are there any imbalances? If so, what might be causing them? How could such imbalances be redressed? What priority should you give to this?

3. Men – what do we do? Assess your current ministry among men. Look at those activities which are specifically aimed at men as well as those which involve both sexes. List the activities and assess honestly how attractive they are to all the men with whom you are in contact - both inside and outside the church.

4. Men at home Identify how many women within your congregation have partners who aren't Christians or regular churchgoers. In what ways would they like support in their hope for their partners to become Christians? (Of course, this also applies to men who come to church without their partners.) This sensitive issue may conceal some deep hurts and emotions just beneath the surface. A simple survey with neat answers may not be enough. In this context you may wish to read Marion Stroud's helpful book *Loving God But Still Loving You* (Scripture Press / CPAS).

5. Male on Sunday - *an outsider's perspective*
Invite a range of men who aren't Christians to give their first impressions of Sunday services and general church life. Be sure to chose men who are as representative of your area as possible. The following form gives a possible approach to 'seeing ourselves as others see us'.

First Impressions Survey *We hope you enjoyed your visit to this church. In order to help us improve our standards of 'visitor-friendliness', we should value your first impressions of us. Please complete this short form and return it to a member of the church staff. Feel free to sign it - or to remain anonymous should you prefer.*

		yes	no	not applicable	comment
The church is	easy to find				
	attractive from the outside				
	welcoming and friendly				
I enjoyed	the whole service				
	the notices				
	the hymns / songs / music				
	the prayers / readings				
	the sermon				
	children's / youth work				
	after the service				

Ideas for improvement

Name (optional)   Date of visit

Thank you very much for your help.

Jesus meets... Nathanael
Read John 1:29-51

On your marks...

Nathanael (1:45) Unlike Andrew, Peter and Philip, Nathanael is not listed as one of the twelve Jesus later called to be his closest disciples. He is mentioned as one of those who went out fishing with Peter after Jesus' resurrection (John 21:2).
Nazareth (1:45) is in Galilee. Galileans were frequently despised by those from Judea. Apparently even fellow Galileans had reason for looking down on Nazareth.

Activity In advance prepare two large pieces of paper. One should show a picture (or rough drawing) of the place where your church meets. The other should have a picture or image representing Jesus. Invite group members to think of a man they know who isn't a Christian. What would this man think about the church and about Jesus? (If the group has more than eight members you may want to consider splitting into pairs or buzz groups for this part of the activity.) Write their responses on the sheets around the relevant picture. Next, select from the responses those which you consider to be 'exclusively male' – in other words, which couldn't have been made by a woman. Underline them in a different colour.

Now discuss:
*   How representative are these comments of men generally?
*   To what extent are the comments true for your church?
*   To what extent are they 'image problems' in the minds of the men outside church?

Get set...

Nathanael meets Jesus because someone he knows speaks about what he has just discovered (1:43-45).
*   How did you first encounter Jesus? Split into pairs to tell briefly your 'story of faith'.
*   Identify any people who played a significant role in your journey to faith. Was he or she an acquaintance, a neighbour, a family member, a friend, a work-mate, minister...?
*   In what ways can we appropriately tell our story, or part of our story, to men who aren't Christians? What sort of events might help a man whom you already know discover more about Jesus?

Nathanael dismissed Philip's claims about Jesus (1:46).
*   What are the negative responses we are likely to receive from men when we talk about Jesus?
*   How can we best handle such responses (1:46)?
*   As we think about ways to speak to men about Jesus, what can we learn from Jesus' first words to Nathanael (1:47)?

Go!

Man to man Invite group members to consider the following question: Is there a man with whom you have regular contact for whom you could start to pray? He doesn't have to be a close friend or family member. It may be better if he isn't. Ask God to make you aware of who your 'contact man' might be. Encourage group members to pray for their 'contact man' regularly.

Pray Spend some time praying together, either in silence or aloud. (Be careful not to put pressure on men who are unaccustomed to praying aloud.) Pray for one another as you look for opportunities to 'be a Philip' to your contact man. Each time you meet, talk about how things have or haven't developed. Help one another to work out ways to be like Philip to them. Be sensitive about confidentiality.

CHAPTER 2

WANTED: REAL MEN

Tom and Jackie have twins. Katie climbs trees and loves sport: 'She's a complete tomboy,' boast her parents. Greg is much quieter: he's happiest when playing with Katie's discarded dolls. Tom and Jackie don't boast about their son. 'It's just a phase,' murmurs Jackie. 'I'll buy him an Action Man,' says Tom.

Why do most of us feel comfortable when we learn that a woman enjoys football or motor-racing, but less so if a man says his hobby is embroidery? There's a shifting borderline dividing acceptable from unacceptable masculine behaviour. For most of us, locating that boundary is a matter of gut-level response, rather than thoughtful consideration. In this chapter we shall look at some of today's most common assumptions about masculinity.

Maleness and masculinity

The birth of our first child was a bewildering experience. But despite twenty-eight hours without sleep, even I could identify the sex of our baby with a casual bleary-eyed glance in the right direction.

In his book *Men and Masculinity* (Hodder & Stoughton), Roy McCloughry identifies maleness as a 'biological given'. (At the same time, of course, it's important to acknowledge very real dilemmas of sexual identity caused by hormonal or chromosome imbalance.) What is not so easily identifiable, says McCloughry, is masculinity – 'the values, expectations and interpretation' attached to being male.

People's understanding of what constitutes masculinity varies widely between nations and across cultures. For example, while working among Muslim people in Italy, I was astonished when a new male friend took my hand as we walked down the street. This is not what *men* do, said my British upbringing. I learned later that my Muslim friend's sense of decorum was equally offended by the accepted European custom of hand-holding between boyfriend and girlfriend.

Standards of masculinity also vary from age to age. For example, just how close was the disciple John to his Master at the Last Supper? The modern-day New International Version of the Bible has the disciple 'reclining next to' Jesus (John 13:23). The older Revised Standard Version speaks of him 'lying close to the breast of Jesus'. The seventeenth-century translators of the Authorized Version had no qualms about picturing the intimacy of the disciple 'leaning on Jesus' bosom'. The last is the more *accurate* translation, but the NIV may be the more *acceptable* translation because of our contemporary Western assumptions about masculinity, and about what is appropriate behaviour between men.

Asking questions

Questions of maleness and masculinity, femaleness and femininity, beg further questions that go to the roots of our sense of identity and worth. Most people would agree that it has been women, rather than men, who have put time and energy into asking such questions in recent years. The last three decades have witnessed a revolution in the way women think of themselves and their role in the home and in the workplace. As a result we are increasingly sensitive to stereotyped views of them.

Is there evidence of men wanting to be similarly inquisitive? Very little – at least not until relatively recently. Visit your local book shop: it's likely you will find a complete section dedicated to contemporary 'women's issues'. I doubt if you will find more than a handful of titles offering similar help to men. Given the lack of serious discussion, it's hardly surprising that we continue to accept many traditional assumptions of what it means to be a 'real man'.

Stereotypical images

What follows is a selection of statements about men. All of them are current in contemporary society. Of course, they are all generalizations: those which strike a chord with some people may seem irrelevant to others. But taken together, they paint a picture of what it means to be a man in the eyes of many people today. Our problems start when we think of them as the *only* way of understanding men.

'Real men stand on their own.' They don't like to appear vulnerable or to ask for help. They solve problems independently. Expressing pain, anguish or uncertainty is not part of normal male behaviour. Disciplined by the referee during the 1990 World Cup semi-final, England footballer Paul Gascoigne broke down and wept. His tearful reaction to his booking provoked massive media attention – all of which reflected the strength of our belief that 'big boys don't cry'.

'Real men are action men.' Their motivation is the 'external' world of action, events and facts. The 'inner world' of reflection, emotion and intimacy is a minor concern. This 'bias to the external' is reflected in the language men use. For example, which is the more 'masculine' statement about buying a bicycle: 'I chose my bike because it has 36-speed Shimano index gears, Reynolds 501 frame and high-impact suspension...' or 'I chose my bike because I want to do my bit for the environment – and cycling helps me get in touch with nature and so enhances my spiritual life'?

'Real men are goal-driven.' They can 'compartmentalize' their lives. This single-minded attitude may extend to their partners. A man may give his full attention to romance during the 'courting' phase of a relationship. But once he has achieved the hoped-for goal, he seems to cross the word 'romance' off his mental 'to do' list, as he moves onto another goal in life.

'Real men like a challenge.' They like succeeding against the odds in the workplace, on the football field, at the annual flower and produce show. At the gym a real man wants to lift more weights than the next man; at the pub, he wants to be able to out-drink his mates. Real men are competitive.

'Real men are achievement-oriented.' We value a man by his achievements, which may include power, promotion, possessions, property, popularity, or physical prowess. What a man *does* matters more than who a man *is*.

'Real men like to be with other men.' They have a strong herd instinct and enjoy attending sports and following pursuits where they are part of the large crowd. The pub is their refuge. But although 'real men' are not solitary, their friendships tend to be superficial – they are wary of intimacy.

'Real men are sexual predators.' In relationships, men take the initiative and expect to be the dominant partner. Despite the seeming success of the 'sexual revolution', the double standard is still alive and well. Witness the fact that our casual description of a sexually predatory male is likely to be 'wolf' or 'stud'. A similarly aggressive woman risks being dismissed as 'slut' – or worse.

'Real men are heterosexual.' A red-blooded male has no doubts about his sexual orientation. Given a 'normal' background and a 'normal' upbringing, a 'normal' boy ought to grow up to be a 'normal' man. If a man doesn't have a partner and children by his mid-thirties, then, surely, there must be something wrong with him.

Caricatures they may be, but these eight attributes combine to provide a standard by which, consciously or otherwise, we assess if someone is a 'real man'. And we rely on stereotypes in church circles just as much as we do in the 'everyday' world. When a speaker is praised as a 'real man's man', we instantly know what the description means: he matches the stereotype of masculinity.

Reality check

The less time we spend reflecting on what it *really* means to be a man, the more likely we are to be swayed by pre-packaged stereotypes. Here are some ways in which behaviour may be influenced by responding to stereotypes rather than to reality.

'Strivers' Some men work hard to embody the stereotype. They want to be considered a 'real man', so they act like one. Their behaviour influences their relationships both at work and in leisure time; in particular their relationships with women.

'Achievers' Other men appear to fulfil all expectations effortlessly. They lead the pack with confidence – the confidence of being unchallenged about their view of what it means to be a man.

'Pretenders' Some may acknowledge inwardly that they are wearing a mask. Such unresolved tension may cause long-term problems.

'Worriers' Some find their failure to match the stereotypical view of masculinity a constant source of anxiety.

'Ignorers' Others are aware of the stereotype, but don't want to aspire to it.

'Rebels' Some positively relish flouting the stereotypical view of masculinity.

Stereotypes, in the end, simply won't do. They give a limited – and limiting – guide to what it means to be a man.

Hoping for the best?

The church's reluctance to think through issues of maleness and masculinity means that we not only accept the stereotypes, we are in danger of reinforcing them. This can spill over into our evangelism among men. Let me describe a fictional, but typical, situation.

Brian, John, Jack, Bill, Joe and Matt are among the small band of adult males who regularly attend Broad Street Church. The leadership team has decided on an 'outreach focus' on men. Eager to portray Christian men as neither weak or wimpish, they book the function room of the Rose and Crown and invite a well-known Christian sportsman to be guest speaker. They encourage all of the church's men to invite their male friends who aren't Christians.

The venue is a pub, the speaker is a footballer. What could have more man-appeal? But let's take a closer look at how Broad Street's strategy works out in practice.

- Brian's recently divorced neighbour never goes to pubs. Will he feel at home in the Rose and Crown?
- John loves sport and avidly supports the local football team. He attends every match with a bunch of mates. He's sure one of his mates, Ron, will be interested in coming along to the Rose and Crown.

Telling stories...

A church in the Midlands had an established men's meeting. Between fifteen and twenty-five men gather in a hotel once a month to hear guest speakers on a range of subjects. Most of the speakers are Christians. Occasionally there are specifically evangelistic events. The majority of those attending are older retired men, but a few younger men make occasional visits. Among the younger group was one of the church leaders, a married man with four children. After attending the men's meeting for some time he found himself increasingly frustrated by its lack of relevance to his daily life.

After some thought he called a meeting for men with the specific intention of exploring links between their faith and day-to-day life in both home and workplace. Twenty-five men turned up, the majority of them from the younger age group. At a follow-up meeting, they decided to form two smaller weekly discussion groups – one meeting early in the morning, the other scheduled for evenings.

A deep level of mutual commitment has grown out of the group members' desire to help one another practise what they were learning during their time together. The benefits have not been limited to the men in the groups. They have found ways to support the leaders of their church and to reach out to other men. The two different approaches to work among men continue to run on parallel tracks, meeting the different needs of men.

- Jack's friend Mike has no interest in sport. Will the speaker appeal to him?
- Bill's high-pressure job in the city leaves him little time for cultivating friendships. His colleague Sam is his only regular contact who isn't a Christian. But Sam, a fellow-commuter, does not live locally. If he accepts Bill's invitation he will have to make a round-trip of more than 100 miles to attend the event at the Rose and Crown.

- Joe is unemployed. Will the meeting boost or undermine his fragile sense of self-worth? Will he have to maintain his usual mask of bravado?
- Matt has only just become a Christian. His brother Mark has been asking questions. Matt thinks he'll be able to invite him along, especially as the Rose and Crown is their local.

Still such a good idea? It certainly seems so for John and his football-fan friend Ron, and also quite possibly for Matt and Mark. But what about Bill, Jack and Brian? All of them seem to have quite valid reasons for giving the event a miss, yet could be made to feel guilty for not turning out. And that would be tragic, because all of them have contact with men who aren't Christians. The event is simply not appropriate for their particular contacts. What needs developing is Broad Street's 'method of evangelism' rather than these men's commitment as Christians. Joe, of course, flags up another area of difficulty. He can cope with a low-cost, church-based men's activity – but his weekly budget won't stretch to buying drinks at the pub.

There are two key issues here:
- Does our men's work reinforce unhelpful stereotypes about what a 'real man' is?
- Does our men's work help the broadest range of Christian men in their desire to share their faith with others, or are we locked into just one potentially limiting model?

Variety show

Of course it is good when one style of event works. Many church-based men's activities are meaningful to a significant number of men. But I am convinced that we need to explore a *variety* of ways of reaching *different* types of men – and that we should develop a sensitivity to the negative effects of allowing stereotypical assumptions to shape our plans. We need to do two things:

Identify current trends amongst men Starting from the simple determination to avoid stereotypes, we need to take a searching look at masculinity today. It's vitally important that we have some understanding of the range of experience and attitudes among contemporary men. Without it we will have little hope of reaching the large number of 'unchurched' men, particularly those aged under forty-five, who have little or no contact with the church or with Christian lifestyles.

Develop parallel tracks for reaching men Having acknowledged that there's no 'catch all' method of reaching men, existing men's meetings should sponsor the development of 'alternative' strategies. Often it is the leaders of the existing work who have positions of authority in a church. They can use this to promote meetings, activities and initiatives that will appeal to men not attracted by the existing activities. In other words, carry on with what will work with John and Matt, but also explore developments that would be appropriate for Bill, Jack, Brian and Joe as well.

In your church there may be an existing, well-established men's group. But however well it's going, it's worth asking whether or not it's attracting only a certain type of man.

As a way forward, any group could consider the following:
- sponsor a new work, through both prayer and financial support.
- identify potential leaders and invite them to discuss innovative ideas.
- ask older men to 'mentor' younger men in the leadership of new groups.

The two (or more) types of work should not be in competition, but should run in parallel. Both are needed to further the work amongst the diverse range of today's men.

Good examples?
How do you react to these two remarks concerning styles of evangelism among men?

'Often, the rather unhelpful model that is held up for Christian men is of individuals who are confident, self-sufficient, capable and successful.' *Roger Murphy, Nottingham University, on research into church-based men's meetings.*

'I've been given responsibility for our men's work. Our monthly evening meeting only appeals to a particular sort of man. I'm aware of several other groups of men for whom this model just isn't appropriate. Yet I feel under pressure to support the "status quo". What should I do?' *Robin, curate in a Midlands parish.*

START HERE

Ideas for developing awareness about men

1. Men watching Accurate data about men in your congregation will help with planning. If you already have a men's meeting, use one of those gatherings to gain the information you would like – but don't forget to canvass those who don't attend such a meeting. It is important to have *all* the men in the congregation involved, including those who are supporters, interested, or simply attenders. Use a questionnaire, or if you have a smaller number of men, you may like to interview them. The following format could be adapted according to your particular situation.

Name _____ Age _____

Employed / unemployed _____ Present / last job _____

Where do you regularly meet men who aren't Christians or churchgoers?

- ☐ At work *(please specify)*
- ☐ Hobbies or interests *(please specify)*
- ☐ Pub *(name)*
- ☐ Other *(please specify)*
- ☐ Clubs *(please specify)*
- ☐ Sports *(please specify)*
- ☐ Neighbourhood

Why do you attend church? (Tick all the statements that apply.)

- ☐ I have an active Christian belief
- ☐ I come to church to support my partner
- ☐ I enjoy the services
- ☐ I've always gone to church – it's a habit
- ☐ I'm curious about Christianity
- ☐ Other *(please specify)*

How long have you been a Christian?

- ☐ Less than two years
- ☐ Between five and ten years
- ☐ Between two and five years
- ☐ More than ten years

Can you identify a man who is not a Christian, for whom you could pray? If so:

What distance does he live from the church?

What major issues is he facing in his daily life?

What sort of event might interest him?

What would you identify as your biggest difficulty when it comes to sharing your faith with other men?

---

2. Jesus meets... Look at the Bible study materials at the end of each chapter of this book. Use them with an existing group, or as the basis of a specially-convened course. The material focuses on how Jesus related to men and on the implications of those encounters for us today.

3. Male agenda Establish a group to explore some issues of what it means to be 'Christ-like' as a man today. The materials in the final section of this workbook (pages 44-48) are designed to provide ideas and resources for running such a group.

4. Man's lot Invite men to contribute to a file of conflicting images of men: photos, headlines, articles, adverts, TV clips, examples from daily life. Create a display of the material to raise awareness of some of the issues men face. Use it as publicity for any men's work you are trying to develop.

Jesus meets... Nicodemus
Read John 3:1-21

On your marks...

Nicodemus (3:1) was a religious and political leader; he was a Pharisee (a strict sect committed to keeping the Jewish law) and a member of the Jewish ruling council (the Parliament of the day). We know that later in Jesus' ministry Nicodemus stood up before the council to challenge them to give Jesus a fair hearing (John 7:50). After Jesus' death he helped to carry his body to the tomb (John 19:38-42).

'Born again' (1:3,7). This phrase can also be translated 'born from above'. Becoming a Christian involves a change so radical that it can only be described as a rebirth (1:5). Sadly, the phrase 'born again' is a 'turn-off' for many people. This is tragic because Jesus used it to emphasize two vitally important truths. First, you can't claim to be a Christian just because you are religious, or good, or born of the right parents, or in the right country. Nicodemus had all of these qualifications and yet still needed to be born again. Secondly, however it happens, God is the one who brings about the rebirth through his Spirit (1:5-8). For some this rebirth will be a dramatic moment that can be given a time and date. For most it will be a gradual process.

Activity Make a photocopy of the list of male stereotypes on page 11. Give each member of the group a copy and invite them to assess the extent to which they agree with each description. Using a scale of one to five, let one represent 'I don't agree at all' and a score of five indicate complete agreement.

Now discuss:
• Where do these stereotypical images come from?
• In what ways are we influenced by them?

Get set...

Nicodemus was a devoutly religious man, and would have been held in high esteem in the community (3:1,10), yet he came to Jesus at night.

Invite group members to discuss the following questions in pairs and then feed back to the larger group.
• Why do some men find it difficult to express thoughts on 'deep' matters, particularly concerning religious faith?

Nicodemus had preconceived ideas about religious matters, and yet was obviously intrigued by Jesus (3:2) he struggled to understand what he was talking about (3:9).
• What ideas do men that you know have about the following subjects?

God
Jesus
Meaning of life
What happens after death?
Sin
Religion
Church

• What is likely to generate interest in Jesus among the men you know?
• As we think about ways to speak to men about Jesus, what can we learn from Jesus' opening words to Nicodemus (3:3)?

Go!

Man to man John 3:16 is one of the most famous verses of the Bible. How would we communicate the meaning of this verse to our contact men in a way that would make sense for them? Discuss this in pairs and then invite group members to share ideas with the whole group.

Pray Spend some time in quiet. Play some appropriate background music if this is helpful. Ask God to identify areas you struggle with as men. Be honest and quietly offer them to God for his forgiveness or help. Thank God for his initiative in reaching out to us. Read Psalm 16 together as an act of trusting God with our lives. In threes, continue to pray for your contact men. Are there any ways God has been prompting you as you pray? You may like to share these with your small group.

CHAPTER 3

MILLENNIUM MEN

So what does it mean to be a man today? It's clear that no single answer is available. And out of our confusion have come a variety of 'ways of being a man'. This chapter will explore several contemporary responses to that central question. We shall also scan some of the background factors that help put these responses in context.

As the century ends, all of the main aspects of life – work, family, security, sexuality and role – are in a state of change. Old certainties are fading (remember the notion of a 'job for life'?), and some men are becoming increasingly sceptical about the image of masculinity that they have inherited.

Others, probably the majority, sense the turbulence of the times through the messages of the mass media – particularly through advertising. TV and newspaper commercials use images of men and women that undermine many traditional assumptions about their roles. For example, they use images of the capable, caring man nurturing his family. Equally popular is the 'power-dressed' executive woman who glides through the corridors of power, firmly exerting her authority over men.

Changing roles

Some changes have been wholly positive, liberating people from inappropriate restraints and prejudices. Others have left people feeling insecure and confused. The fixed roles of the past had certain strengths. Men had a clearer idea of what was expected of them, there was less confusion: they may have had problems, but there was a clearer understanding of the way to deal with problems – even if it meant 'grin and bear it'. Of course, change is stressful for everybody, regardless of age or sex. It's fair to say, though, that recent changes in the specific areas of work and family life have had special significance for men.

Work and employment

Roles have changed and continue to do so.
*   In 1994 forty-five per cent of Britain's paid workforce was female, compared with thirty-seven per cent in 1991. (*Social Focus on Women*, Central Statistical Office, 1995)
*   By 2006 the number of women in the UK's workforce will increase by almost eleven per cent, while the number of men will increase by just over two per cent. (*Employment Gazette*, August 1995)

More and more jobs will be part-time and the majority of these will go to women. So, as companies 'down-size', employees face an increasingly uncertain future. And because traditional expectations die hard, the emerging world of short-term employment contracts poses more of a challenge to men than to women.

Work roles within the home are also changing, though probably at a slower rate. In many modern partnerships the man takes some responsibility for household chores, though in most cases the woman usually does the larger share. What is certain, though, is that the traditional roles of woman as homemaker and man as breadwinner are in a state of flux.

Family

My grandfather would have been horrified at the mere suggestion that he should change a nappy. My father would have done so when my mother wasn't around. Now that I have children of my own, I take it for granted that my wife and I share such delicate manoeuvres equally. Similarly, my grandfather would not have been allowed to be present at the birth of his children. My father would have had a choice. Now, it's an almost unquestioned expectation that a man will be present at the birth of his children. Men are now expected to be far more involved with their children than they were in the past. The developmental experts promote the importance of father-child bonding, and men seem to be following their advice.

However, many men are increasingly sidelined from family life as more and more children are born into single-parent families; the increase in divorce often isolates men from their children. Some children's books no longer include a father in their portrayals of family life – a sign of the times. In some cases, men may simply feel redundant: as one friend of mine said, 'Call me "junk male".'

Increasing pressures

The traditional male roles of provider and protector are no longer clearly defined. So what is 'male identity'? Men used to find theirs in work and in physical strength, but the modern world no longer guarantees a place for these. What is common, though, to most men is the experience of pressure. Wherever I go, I meet men who say: 'I'm stressed.'

Let's take a closer look at some of the important pressure points that affect the lives of today's men.

Stressed-out Steve can't cope: long hours at work, demanding children, unfinished tasks around the home, a marriage that's going flat, friends he never gets to see, an expanding waistline, and never a moment to himself. He's slumped in a chair, asking himself yet again, 'What can I do? There's simply not enough of me to go round.'

Down-sized Dave now has a fixed-term contract. With 'downsizing', he now does the work that, until recently, would have been shared between one and a half, two or even three people. He says: 'When I arrived eight years ago, we had nearly 600 people working here. We are now down to 192.'

Redundant Ron was forty-six when Nuclear Electric made him, and 1000 other employees, redundant. 'It was simple', he said 'they wanted more megawatts per man hour.' Two years, approximately 450 applications and seven interviews later, he landed a job as a dispatch clerk at an annual salary of £8,000. His former salary had been £31,000. 'It's not an experience I'd want to repeat,' he said. The reality, though, is that he may well experience redundancy again before his working life ends.

Confused Clive is the proud dad of a young baby. He plays his part around the home. But he's worried: 'I would like my wife to stay at home and look after Sam, but she wants to go back to work. She thinks I'm being unrealistic, and I can see her point. To be honest, I wouldn't want to stop my work and stay at home. What should I do?'

Depressed Darren is 'third-generation' unemployed. He has two children, but lives with neither of their mothers. Looking around the estate where he lives he sees some men who play the benefits system to their advantage, and others who seem to be its victims. The workforce doesn't need him; his former partners are bringing up his children without his help. He's bored, resentful and has little reason to believe that honesty is the best policy.

Conflicting images

Whenever expectations change and stress-levels increase, uncertainty and conflict usually follow close behind. The voice of traditional expectations says: 'You're a man, so be strong, physically and emotionally. Be aggressive. Don't admit to weakness or vulnerability. Remember, real men don't cry.'

Meanwhile a newer, and increasingly insistent, voice sets a very different agenda: 'You're a *modern* man: you should be in touch with your emotions, tough *and* tender, intimate, vulnerable, close to your partner – a hunk with a heart.'

The fact that men are confused may reflect an equally muddled attitude among today's women. In a perceptive newspaper article, Jane Gordon comments that what women *say* they want of men, and what they *really* want are two very different notions.

'The men we find most attractive, the ones who really excite us, are those who display the most overtly masculine characteristics, not those who do all the ironing, washing up, change the nappies and want to talk endlessly about their innermost feelings... Somewhere between the traditional ideal of the man as dominant provider and the new vision of the domesticated and emasculated New Man lies a compromise that might result in a partnership – one that not just women but also men might want.' ('Even Mr Right gets it wrong', *Daily Telegraph*, 3 July 1996, see page 37.)

So what *does* it mean to be a man today? Most men don't know and some don't care. But all men are affected by changing expectations, whether or not they can identify them. Only someone living in total isolation could fail to be affected by contemporary changes in the worlds of work, family, leisure and entertainment.

Men with masks

The more men concentrate on meeting the demands of the external world, the less time and energy they are likely to have to address inner questions. Roy McCloughry comments: 'Contemporary masculinity is functional and not spiritual, it has more to say about "doing" than "being".' Men chase security, significance and self-worth through what they do, rather than discovering it in who they are. The things on a man's 'to do' list may have changed, but they still promote an image behind which he can hide: 'Look, I've got a good relationship, healthy children, a house, mortgage, car *and* go abroad for my holidays. What do you mean "there's more to life"?' Yet deep down, behind the mask, many men *are* struggling with the thought 'There must be more to life than this.'

Ignoring the spiritual aspect of life doesn't make it go away. The activity of the external world simply floods in to

fill the vacuum. So work becomes the means of maintaining a sense of purpose; relationships become 'support bases' from which we can go out to make further achievements; even sex can become an antidote to the yearning for deep intimacy. In short, all too frequently we trade a higher standard of living for a lower quality of life.

Society's understanding of masculinity is changing. Some changes are for the better, some are not. What really is crucial though, is our response to these changes. Will we use them as an opportunity to discover what it means to be a man made in the image of God? Or will we allow them to cause a retreat into unthinking stereotypes, even if they are Christian ones?

Telling stories...

A church in north-west London, based on a council estate, held occasional men's meetings in the church hall. These usually attracted between ten and fifteen men, most of them from the church, to listen to guest speakers, most of whom were Christians.

They realized they weren't engaging with the working-class men of the estate. After considerable prayer and thought they adopted a new four-point strategy.

Social events based around food, including an opportunity to relax playing a variety of indoor 'pub' games.
Work groups The church hall was shared with the local community. Two men started meeting on Saturday mornings to do repairs. Within six months the number had risen to forty; many of the unemployed men on the estate were willing to lend a hand.
Quarterly evangelistic events These included local men talking about their faith, as well as a contribution from an invited speaker. They took great care with the selection of speakers to ensure they would relate well to this particular group of men.
Small-scale Bible study groups emerged for those who became Christians.

Contemporary responses

Roy McCloughry identifies two specific responses to the changes affecting men today: the 'new man' and the 'wild man'. I have added two further 'types' based on my own observations. Each one is a generalization – people can't be boxed so easily. But, that said, they should help us focus on how many of today's men are reacting to a changing world.

Traditional Man continues as before. He says: 'What's all the fuss about? What's wrong with the way things were?' Traditional Man may be aware that some of the more extreme male stereotypes are unhelpful for those around him as well as for himself – but it's equally likely that he is not. He withdraws into what is familiar and gives little time to all the changes 'out there'. He may be able to maintain his position because many of those around him are also content with the way things are.

Macho Man's response is to assert his power and strength. Sometimes driven by a sense of insecurity, sometimes by a simple desire to fulfil the male stereotype, he displays an aggressive, 'in your face' kind of masculinity. Other men may pursue new ways of being a man, but he won't be influenced by them – he's completely unaware that his combative stance is a classic example of 'over-compensation' to a threatening environment. What is Macho Man's definition of a 'real man'? He may be unwilling to admit it, but he'd agree with the stereotypes of 'real men' in the last chapter (page 11). A popular contemporary development of this can be found in the 'new lad' culture satirized by the TV programme *Men Behaving Badly*.

New Man wants to be different. Looking back, he is appalled when he reflects on men's 'track record' of injustice towards women. He's aware of discrimination in the workplace. He acknowledges that men have neglected their responsibilities as fathers. He seeks to realign himself with new thinking, and takes pride in his

ability to be a part of a 'new order'. New Man is concerned about planetary issues; he takes his share of home chores; he longs for equality and wants to help liberate his partner from the shackles of the past. He wants to be in touch with his inner self.

Newspapers and television, and to a certain extent the advertisers, identify this paragon of 'reconstructed masculinity' as the caring man of the future. *Cosmopolitan* refers to him as the 'hunk with a heart'. In Australia he's a 'SNAG' (Sensitive New Age Guy).

Wild Man is in search of a neglected, deeply powerful, aspect of himself – the warrior within. His chief promoter is Robert Bly, the author of the influential book *Iron John* (Addison Wesley). Investigating men's responses to the feminist revolution, Bly is particularly worried about the emergence of the New Man. He asks: in their concern to right past wrongs, are these sensitive, caring New Men denying profoundly important aspects of themselves? Bly fears that our response to the women's movement has, in fact, emasculated men: in some modern marriages it's almost as if the children are being raised by two women. Bly longs for men to recognize their untapped inner resources of strength and power, to become 'warriors' again. Press and TV have publicized some of the more eccentric aspects of this and have focused on group weekends (usually in a woodland setting) featuring drumming, bivouac building and tearful 'male bonding'.

Bly's aim is not to reassert traditional or 'macho' stereotypes, but to help men discover resources which will unleash their ability to become their 'real selves'. Some of his thinking has influenced the work of Richard Rohr, an American Franciscan friar who emphasizes the need for men to make a journey *through* the recognition of the feminine within themselves to the tapping of the 'deep masculine' within.

Ideas for understanding the challenge of change

- **Pressure points** What are the main pressures affecting the men with whom you have contact? Copy the chart below. List the pressure points and then try to identify what the church could do to alleviate these pressures?

Name	Home pressures	Work pressures	Possible church response

- **Masculine tendencies** Look at the four types of response to change listed in this chapter. Think about the community in which your church is set. Can you identify a prevailing response to change amongst its men? Are there other categories you would like to add? What are the implications of these particular reactions to change for life in your community?

- **Childless fathers** How many men within the congregation are divorced or separated and have little or no access to their
children? What are the issues such men face? Is there anything the church can do to support them?

- **Single issues** Invite single men within the church to comment on their position. You can probably do this through personal conversations – but you may also wish to try holding a meeting for the church's single men. What are the particular needs of single men? How can these be met?

- **Behind the masks** A recent survey suggested that some men have had significant spiritual experiences but are afraid to talk about them with anyone. These experiences include answered prayer at a time of crisis and an awareness of a longing for inner peace prompted by watching a child at play. Invite men to write anonymously about such experiences. Do this via the church magazine, or through house groups. Use the contributions in a men's newsletter or as discussion starters in a men's group.

Jesus meets... a blind beggar
Read Luke 18:35-43

On your marks...

'Blind man... begging' (18:35) Such a person would be considered something of an outcast within the Jewish society of Jesus' day. Yet despite his disability, he sees very clearly when it comes to spiritual issues. For Jesus to commend his faith would have been quite a shock for the crowd; many of whom may have thought his condition was an indication of divine disapproval because he had no faith in God, or had in some way angered God.

Activity Think about some of the changes that the last hundred years have brought. Use the chart to list some of the differences in work life and home life that might have affected three generations of a family across the span of this century.

	Work	Family
Grandfather (Born 1910)		
Father (Born 1940)		
Son (Born 1970)		

Discuss:
- What have been the most difficult aspects of change for each generation to cope with?
- What do we think will be the changes affecting our children as they come to adulthood during the opening decades of the next century?

Get set...

As one who knew the pressure of having to live on the margin of his society, the blind beggar is shunned by the crowd (18:39). Jesus, who is only passing through, stops in the middle of the whole crowd to meet him (18:40).
- How does your church respond to people today who, for whatever reason, don't meet with general acceptance?
- Are there ways we stop men in particular from coming to Jesus?
- In what ways can we act like Jesus to them, not like the crowd?

The beggar says to Jesus, 'Lord I want to see' (18:41).
- What do you think men today would identify as their greatest need, desire or hope?
- Imagine they were to express this to Jesus, like the beggar on the road. How do you think Jesus would respond? (You may also like to think about how you would answer these two questions for yourself.)
- As we think about ways to speak to men about Jesus, what can we learn from Jesus' first words to the beggar (18:41)?

Go!

Man to man Can you identify any men who are regarded as somehow socially awkward or unwelcome? How can we express Christ-like love and acceptance towards such people? In what ways can those of us who are fathers model Christ-like qualities to our sons? Be as specific and practical as you can. Think about your contact man. What do you think he would identify as the greatest need in his life? Is there anything you could do to clear a path towards Jesus for him?

Pray Spend some time praying for grandfathers and fathers. As you pray be aware of any unhelpful attitudes towards them, and if necessary confess them to God. Pray also for the sons of those within the group. In groups of three continue to pray for your contact men.

CHAPTER 4

MEN BEHAVING 'GODLY'

It had been a full day. Working together we had explored a variety of ways of reaching today's men. The men on the course, of varied ages and backgrounds, had all contributed well. As they prepared to leave, one of them expressed his discontent: 'It all seems too psychological. Why don't you just teach men they are sinners who need to repent?' Later, another man sidled up to me and said: 'This has been the most liberating day.'

I've had other equally opposite-seeming reactions on many of the occasions when I've presented similar material. Now I find I'm grateful for both: it's encouraging to discover that many people appreciate the opportunity to explore the 'big issues' of contemporary masculinity. But I'm also happy to be reminded that such exploration needs to be tied in to our overall purpose: the task of introducing men to Jesus Christ.

The church is currently better at reaching women than men. So it seems obvious that we need to address specific issues of masculinity if we are to help contemporary men to discover who they are in relationship to a holy and loving God. Repentance and faith are both crucially important. The gospel has not changed, but the way we help men to hear it does change.

It's for this reason that we must be prepared to put ourselves under the microscope. Are we aware of the thought-forms, attitudes and assumptions which prevent contemporary men from hearing the gospel? And while our message remains unchanging, what aspects of our current practice should we reassess if we are to reach today's men?

Start with Jesus

Acknowledging that there's a challenge to be met is the first step. Next comes the question, 'How should we respond?' The search for an answer begins, I'm certain, with Jesus. How did he model what it means to be a man? How did he relate to people in general, and men in particular?

Jesus is a 'role model' of perfect humanity God created human beings in his image. Tragically that likeness is now broken because of humankind's rebellion against God – we have decided that we know better than God how to live in his world. As a result our relationship with God is harmed: people are unsure of God's existence and unaware of his purpose for their lives. Our relationships with one another are equally damaged – a glance at today's newspaper headlines is usually reminder enough. Fractured existence is painful; our natural reaction to pain is to take avoiding action. One of our basic strategies for pain-avoidance is the wearing of masks, so that we can present an acceptable image to other people – and often to ourselves as well.

Telling stories...

A church in the Manchester area runs men's breakfasts. Realizing that stress is an important issue for many of the men who attend, the organizers planned a breakfast, with a guest speaker, around the theme of 'Stress, stress and more stress.' During the subsequent question and comment session, a retired doctor said: 'When I was a young man I had to work 115 hours a week, and we were on a pittance of pay.'

Later several of the younger men in the group confided in the speaker: they found repeatedly that the older men in the group failed to understand the pressures they were under. One of them said: 'That's why we were so pleased about this subject being addressed. It was easy to invite our colleagues along. We are all stressed out of our brains!'

Jesus came to restore humanity's broken image through his death on the cross – and in the process he 'modelled' for us perfect humanity. He had no need to hide behind masks. He was secure in his relationship with his Father and with other people. He was secure both in *who* he was and in *what* he was to do.

- He was able to give *and* receive service: by washing his friends' feet (John 13:1-17), and by allowing a women of ill repute to wash his feet (Luke 7:36-50).
- He was able to express anger *and* compassion: he took a whip to the Temple money-changers who cheated people in his Father's house (Luke 19:45-46); he wept over the city of Jerusalem and its people's failure to appreciate the significance of his presence among them (Mark 8:34-38) – and showed amazing tenderness to those who failed him (John 21:15-19).
- He was able to accept women gladly as those who supported him in his work (Luke 8:1-3), as well as men.
- He was able to touch with complete tenderness, and challenge with utter ferocity. He took the deaf and dumb man aside, putting his fingers into his ears and touching his tongue, (Mark 7:31-37). His words of challenge to the Pharisees make grim reading, (Luke 11:37-53).
- He was able to teach with power and authority (Mark 1:27; 6:2), and to speak words of love and gentleness (Mark 5:34; 10:13-16; 10:46-52).

Jesus is the ultimate hero, the perfect role model. Here is where we find what it means to be a real man – he is a true 'men-tor'.

Telling stories...

Five men meet four times a year. They are all in their thirties, and share a similar work interest. They meet for honest exploration of issues affecting their lives. One member of the group writes: 'The level of commitment and openness is unparalleled in my experience. It has become one of the most significant developments in my adult life.'

'For me Jesus is the ultimate hero. He is fully human and fully divine and is therefore a bridge by which I can understand both. If I want to know about God I ask "What is Jesus like?" If I want to grow as a human being I ask "How can I be more like Jesus?"'

Roy McCloughry, *Men and Masculinity*, Hodder & Stoughton, page 134.

How did Jesus relate to people?

Jesus didn't allow people to set his agenda For Jesus, *being* with his heavenly Father preceded *doing* things for his heavenly Father (Luke 3:21-22; 4:42-44; 5:16). His perspective and his priorities were based on his relationship with God – they were not the result of day-to-day reactions to the clamouring crowds. This is a vital starting point. Jesus was secure in who he was, and, therefore, was confident in what he had to do.

There are many demands facing those who want to see men respond to Jesus. There is much happening in our society which may cause us concern. But if we don't start by searching for God's perspective and priorities, we will be in danger of adopting a reactive, 'bandwagon' approach to ministry. Jesus took 'time out' to be with God. We need to do the same.

Jesus was deeply concerned for people as individuals He didn't have a formula. Nowhere in the Gospel accounts is there any impression of people being 'processed' through an encounter with Jesus. He understood people, appreciating their needs and how they ultimately needed to respond to him. He comforted the broken and despised; he challenged the proud and the self-satisfied. He invited people to respond to him in different ways, according to what would be appropriate for them at the time. (For further examples see the Bible Explorations at the end of each chapter.)

If we want to encourage men to become followers of Jesus, we should beware of simplistic solutions. Different men will require different approaches. The following three questions may help.

- **What does God want us to do?** Having recognized that 'we ought to be doing something about men', we shouldn't rush into making plans without spending time with God to discern his perspective and priorities. Similarly, it is all too easy to see something working successfully in one place and to assume that it can be transferred with equal effect to another situation.

- **Who are we trying to reach?** Having agreed that understanding today's men is important, who are the men we are specifically trying to reach? There are likely to be a number of possibilities in any one area, so start with men the congregation already know. Where do they meet these men? What are their concerns in life? What would be a good way to provide opportunities for them to encounter Jesus?

- **Where would Jesus want to lead them?** Becoming a Christian is not the end of a process: it's the start of a lifelong journey. Jesus calls us to be like him. He wants to help us live without masks and discover the freedom of being real to ourselves. He longs to heal and to help us at the deepest possible level. This is no 'New Age' programme of 'self-actualization'; we don't become Christ-like through finding ourselves, but through the often painful process of dying to ourselves. Jesus asks us to be willing to serve, even to suffer, for the purposes of God in a broken and disturbed world. How can we structure our work among men in such a way that we fulfil a vision for Christ-like men?

One more burden?

Becoming a Christian should be an amazing liberation. For many people it is. Sadly, though, the real-life experience of many men is not quite so positive. All too often a new-found faith can also add a further item to an already long list of 'things that are expected of me as a successful, confident man'. The unspoken message that many men receive may go roughly as follows: 'Now that you are a Christian you should be leading a confident and triumphant Christian life where you can at last overcome those temptations which you have been struggling with for years.' Men are exhorted to be 'the men God wants them to be'. Without meaning to, we often 'buy into' a far-from-biblical standard of masculine achievement – a Christianized version of what our society accepts as true masculinity.

Some of our most favoured methods of doing 'men's work' may unconsciously reinforce this image. Are we unintentionally encouraging men to keep their 'I'm doing fine' masks firmly in place?

Jesus came to free us from all that holds us back from being the unique people he made us to be. That means that Christian men will come in all sorts of shapes and sizes, from all sorts of backgrounds and experiences. It does not mean all men will express their faith in exactly the same way. It does mean that we will all need to submit our own preferences for what we think it means to be a Christian man to Jesus, who will sift through them and change us day by day, bit by bit.

This is the journey God invites all men to travel – to move from stereotypical images of masculinity towards a 'Jesus model' of being a man. It's a journey that starts with commitment and moves on through the often painful process of becoming like Christ. How do we help today's men start – and persist in – that journey? That's what the next two chapters are about.

Telling stories...

At All Saints, Cottenham, the vicar invites local men who work from home to a monthly lunch at the vicarage. Before ordination Iain worked for Lloyds of London as an adjuster for marine insurance claims. Finding he missed the companionship of office life, he started inviting a few home-based men to a simple lunch. The meeting has grown through personal invitation, rather than as a result of advertising. Iain follows each invitation with a letter giving details of the group and outlining the three basic facts of how it operates:

Come as you are.

The lunch will last for one hour, but you may leave earlier if you wish.

Don't worry if you are unexpectedly prevented from attending a meeting.

Ian sends out a reminder during the week before each lunch. He includes an RSVP to help him plan catering. He recently invited a local Christian business man to speak at a Sunday service on the theme of faith and work. He invited his group of men to the service and to lunch afterwards. Many accepted.

START HERE

An idea for assessing use of time

26

Time Managers Is the church placing too many demands on people's lives? What should the basic commitment to the life of the church be? How is this communicated to people within the church and those who start to attend? How does the church adjust its expectations on people according to changes in life circumstances? Invite the men of the church to fill in a time chart. Be careful not to add feelings of guilt to already over-stretched men. It might help to tell those who are going to fill in the form that its aim is to relieve pressure on them.

Activity	Number of nights per week
Working	
At home with family	
At home alone	
Out with family	
Out with church friends	
Out with non-church friends	
Playing sport	
Doing voluntary work	
In church meetings or groups	
Other	

Weekends

Use the categories above to outline activities on the past four weekends.

	morning	afternoon	evening
Weekend 1			
Weekend 2			
Weekend 3			
Weekend 4			

Jesus meets... Zacchaeus
Read Luke 19:1-10

On your marks...

'Chief tax collector' (19:2) The Roman occupational force enlisted local people to collect taxes. They were generally disliked because they creamed off an 'extra' percentage for themselves. So far Luke has portrayed tax collectors in a favourable light (3:12; 7:29; 15:1; 18:10), but has generally portrayed rich men with disfavour. There is an interesting ambiguity of connection here. A challenge to stereotypes!

'I must stay at your house today' (19:5). Hospitality was an important part of Jewish culture. To stay or eat with people indicated your willingness to stand alongside them, to be identified with them. Hence the crowd's horror that Jesus would be the guest of a 'sinner'.

Activity Case study: as an RAF pilot, Greg was in what many would see as a real man's job. But Greg felt he didn't match the stereotypes of what it means to be man. 'I think my struggle can best be summed up in the words "not fitting". I don't enjoy sports – so I don't fit. As someone with creative gifts, some men tend to stereotype me as gay. I'm not, so I don't fit there either. As a Christian I don't feel I fit in church. The whole thing feels too feminine.' Yet Greg finds Jesus attractive as a role model. 'He is a man in control without having to tell everyone. He doesn't wield his power to stamp his authority. I respect him for that.'

Discuss:
- How do you react to Greg's comments?
- What would you say to Greg to help him to 'fit in'?

Get set...

The people thought of Zacchaeus as a sinner (19:7).
- Do we alienate men by the way we act as individuals or as a congregation?
- What would people identify as sin today? How do these things compare with what Jesus would identify as sin?
- What are some of the particular 'sins' which men struggle with?

- Are there any additional sins we struggle with as Christian men? How can we help each other deal with these?
- How can we better reflect Jesus' attitude towards those who are 'sinners'?

Zacchaeus responded to Jesus' presence by a change of attitude and by making amends (19:8). Jesus affirmed that salvation had come to his house (19:9-10).
- What are the particular difficulties men may have in admitting they have done wrong? How can these be overcome?
- Having acknowledged past wrongs what, if it is appropriate, can we do to make amends?
- What has salvation meant to us in the past? What might it mean in the future in terms of our understanding of what it means to be a man?
- As we think about ways to speak to men about Jesus, what can we learn from Jesus' first words to Zacchaeus (19:5)?

Go!

Man to man Ask group members to consider if there is anyone with whom they need to make amends. You may want to use a period of quiet prayer for this purpose. If you feel it's appropriate, invite group members to split into twos or threes to pray about the issues and situations raised by this activity.

Invite each group member to think about his contact man. Ask the following questions. Which of the categories discussed seems most applicable to him? How can you affirm the strengths of his particular background? What practical difference do you think it would make to him if he became a Christian?

Pray Offer to God your own personal background. In silence, give space for thanksgiving, confession and recognition of the need to make amends. If it is appropriate, talk about your thoughts and pray for one another. Pray for your contact men.

CHAPTER 5

MAN TO MAN

Jack and I were chatting about strategies for reaching men. Obviously disheartened, he said: 'Take my father. He's not yet a Christian; he's a fairly average man. But he doesn't go out much, doesn't have many male friends and rarely goes inside a pub. I've never come across any outreach activity I'd be really comfortable inviting him to.'

Bob is a member of a lively evangelical church. In answer to my question about their men's group, he said: 'They are a nice enough bunch, but they are sport crazy. For me, having the majority of men's events based around watching or participating in sport isn't very helpful. Nor is it for my friends who aren't Christians – we're just not into sport. I've stopped going. So have a number of others I know.'

Tony is a young married man with three children. His church is planning a special period of outreach to men. He told me: 'I'm up to my neck with pressure – at work and at home. My only real contact with men who aren't Christians is at work – and that's twenty-four miles away. I can't really expect my colleagues to accept an invitation to an evening event that's miles away from their home patch.' Tony was left wondering how his church was supporting him in his day-to-day witnessing.

Tony and Bob both want to share their faith, but they find the existing men's programmes either inappropriate or unhelpful. I wonder how many other Christian men are in similar positions.

Is it really any more 'masculine' for men to meet over a pint than it is for them to meet to try out their pizza-making skills? Is it more manly for them to get together to watch a rugby match than to discuss issues of being a father? Is it really more masculine to listen to a Christian business man talk about his successful career, than it is to meet in someone's home to discuss the realities of short-term contracts, workplace ethics and unemployment?

If we want to see men respond to Jesus' call on their lives, how can we structure our evangelism strategies in order to reach as wide a variety of men as possible? Let's explore the following three ideas.

1. Think 'network' as well as neighbourhood

Evangelistic strategies based solely on the local community ignore the realities of many contemporary lifestyles. How can we develop strategies which recognize the fact that many men have their most positive contacts at a considerable distance from the church's immediate neighbourhood? Here are three hints.

Explore 'relational' evangelism as well as event-based evangelism Outreach that's centred around special events has an obvious drawback. It fosters the idea that evangelism is an add-on activity for the church – an extra for those who are interested in 'that sort of thing', or who have particular skills in that area. There's an underlying assumption that people should develop friendships to 'feed' the church's programme of events – and of course there's a built-in element of guilt for those who find themselves too busy with work or family to build new relationships.

Telling stories . . .

Sean meets Graham most weeks early in the morning to work out what it means to be a follower of Jesus in daily life. Graham has recently become a Christian, and faces many questions about his faith and work. He says: 'Am I no longer meant to fight for my ideas in the office? Should I still make people redundant? How am I to handle the go-getting, self-seeking, aggressive members of my team? How should I relate to female colleagues without being sexist or stand-offish?'

Pairing Christian men so that they can engage with real-life issues can be a practical way of developing support and mutual encouragement. A church in south-east England currently has eighty men meeting in pairs: they set their own agendas and arrange time and frequency of meetings on a 'what suits us' basis.

Events, of course, will always have an important role – but I should like to promote an alternative perspective. Shouldn't we be helping men in the relationships they already have with other men? By challenging men to make *new* friendships, we can unintentionally belittle the importance of their network of existing contacts. These people (at work, at the sports club, on the commuter train) may not be close personal friends – but does that really matter? It's possible to relate well to people, without feeling obliged to build the contact into a close friendship.

Not every man is an evangelist, but every Christian man is called to play his part in evangelism. Most men are already in contact with men who aren't yet Christians. These relationships are the best place to start. It's here that we should be helping men to think and behave evangelistically.

Equip men to share their faith wherever they are
Sharing our faith is not a 'special activity' – it's an attitude at the heart of our faith. This attitude should pervade everyday life. For this reason we should be helping Christian men relate their faith to their daily lives, and to the men with whom they have regular contact.

There are many ways to help this 'equipping' process. Here are some of them:

- **The church's 'philosophy of ministry'** What priority is given to reaching those who aren't Christians? Do we talk at all about the importance of outreach, and if we do is it really in terms of 'outreach' rather than 'ingrab'?
- **The church's teaching ministry** Are sermons, home group programmes and youth and children's materials addressing the real-life issues of men and boys within the congregation?
- **Example of church leaders** Do the church's male leaders have any links with men who aren't Christians? I was speaking at a men's breakfast; one table was filled by men the minister had contacted through his 'out of hours' social activities. With the minister practising what he preached, the fact the church was growing didn't surprise me at all.
- **Training** Many people are fearful when it comes to sharing their faith because they simply don't know what to say. Does the church provide practical help with faith-sharing? Is such training appropriate for a variety of personalities and circumstances?

Telling stories...

'People for People' meets on a large retail park outside Bristol. The vision of two men, a businessman and a local Baptist minister, People for People exists to support Christians within the working community. Although membership is open to women, the majority of those attending are men.

They meet on Fridays to discuss issues of faith and work, and Tuesdays to pray about particular concerns. At relevant times through the year they hold evangelistic events. 'It's been slow and hard work,' says Peter, one of the founders, 'but we've a real vision for equipping Christians to relate faith to their working life.'

Resource activity in the places where men are This may involve helping groups of men to plan activities at their place of work, with the minister or other church leaders doing the travelling. It may mean helping Christian men from several churches and workplaces get together at a central location, which may not be a church. It may mean evangelists commuting from a church to a person's place of work. It may mean providing new ways for men to meet within the local community.

2. Think strategically as well as specifically

The vast majority of men in a congregation are in contact with some men who aren't yet Christians. It's unlikely that one single style of event will be appropriate to all of these contacts. Try to plan a range of events, as part of a carefully worked-out programme. Identify particular groups of men and provide what would be most appropriate for them. An older group for retired men may have a completely different agenda and format from a group of young men struggling with parenthood. And there may be very different outlooks and concerns within an age group: even though it has a single destination, the journey into faith takes many routes. Here are a few suggestions.

Social events Simple events which bring men together in a warm and welcoming atmosphere are the best. These may have no set agenda: for example, a walk, a gathering in someone's home, a chat over a pint in a pub, lunch in the canteen at work. Or they may have an agenda, often with a specific outcome: for example, car maintenance, laying concrete, learning to play golf or to cook, paint or draw, going bird watching, attending a match. It's a good idea to aim for a variety of small-scale activities that address a wide spectrum of interests, rather than to concentrate on occasional big events.

Social activities have a built-in problem: after achieving hoped-for success, there's the inevitable question, 'What next?' Some respond by introducing a new element to the format. For example, I heard of a group that met to play badminton. Encouraged by a steady increase in numbers the leaders decided to include an 'epilogue' for the badminton session that coincided with the church's outreach week. This was not a good idea. The players were not impressed by the unexpected addition of a talk to their otherwise enjoyable evening. They felt as if they were being 'got at'. Several of them stopped attending. It would have been much better to invite the club members to a separate activity, leaving those who weren't ready to continue enjoying the sports evening in its normal format.

Practical activities Many men who are wary of church services or socials will happily take part in practical projects. One church organized a large-scale event for their local community. It was called 'It's a Winter Knockout'; the teams were mixed groups of church members and neighbourhood contacts. A planning group was needed to devise the games and make the equipment. Two men who weren't Christians became involved because of particular skills they had to offer. They worked closely alongside church members, both men and women. Within a few months both of them started attending church regularly.

Of course, it's important to be completely honest with people we contact in this way. It would be disastrous to leave a person feeling that the church is more interested in the usefulness – and free availability – of his skill, rather than in him as a person. Similarly, it would be unfortunate if the church found itself in the position of being 'under an obligation' to an enthusiastic volunteer.

Events with specific Christian content Aim for a variety of activities which are suited to your situation. Men's breakfasts may work well in some places but be a disaster elsewhere. Try to build a sense of progression through your programme of activities. A good programme will incorporate a range of approaches in terms of style, format, and content: films, music, sport, cooking, art, talks, debates, game shows, interviews, wine tasting, quizzes, skittles, open agenda groups, and many more can all be used as a way of presenting the Christian faith. However, once you hit a winning style, use it for all it's worth.

Groups and courses on men's issues Recent years have seen the development of men's groups reflecting the growth of a secular 'men's movement'. Some churches have promoted similar groups, offering men a safe place to explore 'men's issues' from a Christian perspective. These groups can be a place where people work at a fairly deep level on what it means to be a man. See pages 44-48 for materials that could resource a series of meetings in this vein. Topics for exploration include employment and unemployment, family and parenting, ethics, decision making, dealing with failure, use of time, money, anger, sex, temptation, and stress.

At this point it's worth asking if single-sex groups are always appropriate? A man in his early thirties came up to me after a men's meeting. He said: 'I'm fed up. Everyone assumes that men only "open up" when they are alone with other men. That's not my experience. I find they keep the masks clamped on. If anything, they use the fact that women aren't present to shore up their deeply-felt male prejudices.' Clearly, his men's meeting had a long way to go. It's important to be sensitive to the concerns some men have about single-sex groups, and it may be right to develop work which will address men's issues in a mixed-sex context. For example, it would be possible to plan a mixed meeting addressing a particular topic, with separate men's and women's discussion groups during the session.

Ten Top Tips for Effective Evangelistic Events

- Establish and maintain an atmosphere which will be 'unchurched-friendly'.
- Meet in non-church venues.
- Ensure the content is relevant.
- Develop a culture of excellence, doing the best you can with what you have.
- Men bring men to events – so equip and inspire your church men to invite others.
- Don't give out church notices, only information that is relevant for the visiting man.
- Develop a sense of belonging. Invite men to comment on the event through appropriate feedback.
- Give value to the event. If charging makes it seem worth attending, subsidize those who can't afford it.
- Ask yourself, 'Where would a man who is interested in taking things further go from here?'
- Don't over-stretch yourselves. Events at four- or six-monthly intervals are more likely to be sustainable than monthly ones.

---

3. Think 'process' as well as result

We long to see men become Christians, and to go on from there to become committed life-long followers of Jesus. That's why our planning must look beyond the wished-for goal of the 'decision for Christ' to the ongoing challenge of discipleship. Two issues are likely to confront us during the process.

Defining model It's possible for a church to have a method of evangelism that helps people come to Christ. That must be good news, mustn't it? But what if that style of evangelism promotes a less-than-Christlike image of what it means to be a man? For example, reaching Macho Man may involve strategies which don't exactly challenge his views about what it means to be a man. Ongoing work with him should both affirm his strengths and help him move on, through the work of the Holy Spirit, to a more Christ-centred understanding of his masculinity. We engage with men by starting where they are. We have to ensure that they are given every help in travelling on to where Jesus wants them to be.

Part of the answer lies in our understanding of what it means to be a local gathering of Christian people. It is good for men to rub shoulders with men from different backgrounds and generations who have different experiences and ideas about what it means to be a man. The aim is to learn from one another and to grow together in Christ. We should avoid the assumptions that identify mature Christian manhood with safe middle-class behaviour. Too often churches have been guilty of drawing working-class men away from their roots, to the extent that they find it difficult to share their faith with people in their 'home community'.

Defining moments Some people can identify a specific place and time (a 'crisis') when they became a Christian. Others may be unable to be so precise, but can still be equally certain they are on a journey of committed discipleship (a 'process'). The former is often typified by Paul's experience on the Damascus Road, the latter the experience of the two disciples on their journey to Emmaus. There needn't be any tension between crisis and process. Even on the road to Emmaus there were significant 'defining moments' for the two disciples as Jesus 'broke open' the scriptures and broke the bread.

In our evangelism strategy we need to give opportunity for defining moments. These are not limited to the call to commitment at the end of an evangelistic talk, though such a challenge may be appropriate. The key is to work out when, where, and how such significant moments are best introduced into the ongoing programme of work amongst men.

Ideas for identifying a place to start

- **Keep in touch** As you move from analysis to action, ask for God's guidance so you may know his purposes for your church. You may want to issue a prayer leaflet which invites the congregation to pray about the work among men. Make sure the leaflet has a response slip so that anyone who senses some prompting from God with regard to work among men can get back to you. You could hold a half-night of prayer, even a day of prayer, specifically about your men's work. There is a Women's World Day of Prayer, so why not a men's equivalent?

- **Look around** Take some time to assess the various resources which are available to help you focus on work among men. Some of them are listed at the back of this workbook. If you don't have a budget for purchasing resources, see if you can borrow any from nearby churches, or try Diocesan resource libraries.

- **Review** Study the material you have gained from the previous sessions, along with the briefing paper of this chapter. Identify key trends from the questionnaires and discussions concerning men. How might these influence your thinking about the way to help men both in and outside the church respond to Jesus?

- **For services rendered** Hold a special service which celebrates what is good about being a man. Of course you would have to be careful about being sexist, or falling into the trap of celebrating the very stereotypes which are unhelpful – but there is much for which to be thankful.

- **Men of God** Take some time to research some Old Testament men. Either use the material for some Sunday teaching, or develop some Bible studies. These stories provide significant insights into ordinary life. For example:

  Moses, a man coping with the results of anger and a sense of inadequacy.
  Joshua, facing an impossible task.
  Samson and failure.
  David, the adulterer.
  Elijah and his struggle with depression.
  Job and his questions.

Jesus meets... the thief on the cross
Read Luke 23:32-49

On your marks...

'Crucified' (23:33) Crucifixion was a particularly brutal, drawn-out form of execution. The victim struggled for breath underneath the hot sun and through the cold night. Jesus wasn't unique in being crucified – thousands of others suffered a similar fate. What was unique was the significance of his death. One scholar puts it like this: 'The cross highlights both the amazing love of God and the appalling nature of sin.' 'Amazing love', because as God he was prepared to become a man and die unjustly for each one of us. The 'appalling nature of sin', because God sees the consequences of sin as so terrible, tragic and permanent that he is prepared to make the ultimate sacrifice to make it possible for human beings to be forgiven and allowed a new start.

Activity 'Wanted - a real man.' In threes and fours try to write a specification for a 'real man'. Have some fun. If someone is artistic, ask him to make a drawing. If not, try to describe what he should look like. List his attributes, define his ambitions, describe his character.

Discuss:
- How does the description compare with Jesus?
- How can we help one another to live up to Jesus' example?

Get set...

We know little about the two men crucified beside Jesus. What we do know is that one of them feared God (23:40), accepted his punishment as just (23:41), and saw in Jesus someone who was different (23:41). The other thief mocked him.

- The thief asks Jesus to remember him when he comes into his kingdom (23:42).
- What would have inspired his request?
- What are the implications of this request for all people?
- What should we say to a man who says (or implies): 'I'm too busy at the moment to think about Jesus', or 'Maybe I'll have a deathbed conversion'?

- Which qualities of Jesus' life would attract men to him today?
- How can we help men we know to see these qualities clearly?
- As we think about ways to speak to men about Jesus, what can we learn from his only recorded words to the thief on the cross (23:43)?

Go!

Man to man In pairs discuss the question, 'What does Jesus' death on the cross means for you?' We often talk about the cross being central to our faith. How would you explain that to a person who doesn't share your faith? How would you explain the significance of the cross in a way that would make sense to your contact man? Can you think of any helpful contemporary illustrations. Share your ideas with the larger group.

Pray Create an opportunity for the group to express gratitude to God for what Jesus means to them. You may like to write a group psalm of thanksgiving, including in it all the key areas you want to say thank you to God for. Read Luke 23:32-49 slowly. In the quiet invite the group to imagine themselves at the scene. What impressions do they receive? How do they feel? What would Jesus say to them if he was to look down from the cross and speak to them. Then listen to a song about the cross (for example, 'Such love', 'When I survey', 'Lord, I lift your name on high', 'There is a redeemer'), and talk about your reflections on what Jesus has done on the cross for you.

- In threes, pray for your contact men in the light of the above meditation.

CHAPTER 6

MANZONE

'I hate all this. I'm fed up with having to sing soppy songs about Jesus. Why does worship feel such a girlie thing? I love singing on the terraces, but I loathe singing in the pews.' This outburst was not from a casual visitor to church; it was from a Christian man who attends every Sunday.

At the start of this workbook we considered some of the obstacles preventing many men from becoming Christians. We identified one of these as the Sunday gatherings we often refer to as church. If we long to see men turn to Christ, we have to face the fact that becoming a Christian involves becoming a 'member of the family'. How can we make sure the family knows how to integrate men, rather than leave them out in the cold?

At your service

Let's begin with the Sunday service. For many this is the most apparent expression of the local church. Let's take a journey through an 'average' service. Some of the suggestions that follow are cosmetic, but that does not belittle their importance – people tend to base judgements on first impressions. Other comments are to do with matters at the heart of the way we 'do' church, and may not be so easy to change.

Arrival First of all, is the church easy to find? Clear signposts really do help. Next, you have to find the way in. I once had the embarrassing experience of spending ten minutes trying to find the entrance to a large Victorian church.

Welcome This can be visual as well as verbal. On occasions I've observed people being ignored on entering a church. And I've seen others, often men, welcomed in such a way as to suggest surprise that they should have turned up at all. To help give a more representative image of its membership, a church in the West Midlands has started involving younger men in its welcome team.

Notices What about the notice boards? Are they neat and tidy? Are all the posters for women's events, or feminine in style? What about the notice sheet? How many notices refer to events that are mainly for women? Are there notices that say to a man that things are happening here for him?

Songs There is a tension here: we want to help men to be able to express appropriate intimacy to God in songs, but many men find doing so very difficult. Some find it hard enough to say 'I love you' to their partners, so it should be no surprise that to say 'Jesus, I love you' does not necessarily come easily. It's important to select and introduce songs carefully. If there are action songs, introduce them in such a way that it is clear people don't have to take part.

Any discussion of styles of music is bound to be controversial. All the same, as far as men are concerned, many of our contemporary worship songs are set to music which is very difficult to sing. It's often pitched too high, and is a long way removed from the contemporary music scene.

Graham Cray, theological college principal and popular music expert, says, 'In many churches we are still using music based on the rock melodies of the seventies band the Eagles, and we think we are up to date!' For all its weaknesses, the Nine O'clock Service in Sheffield used songs which were both contemporary in music style and used language which would have been understood on the street.

It helps to have a balance in the male-to-female ratio of music leaders. I was recently in a London church where all of the singing group were women. I wondered what this communicated to the average man – that singing in worship is a 'woman's thing'?

Liturgy Good liturgy provides shape, pattern and rhythm for worship, making it into a familiar, shared experience. It retells the story of faith, but should do so in a way which relates to the story of life. Liturgy includes mystery and majesty. Are there ways to use liturgy to affirm men in their place in God's purposes? We need to discover a 'liturgical language' that is meaningful and 'resonant' for men. For example, in his book *Called to Account* (Hodder & Stoughton), Richard Higginson provides a liturgy on work. Of course, that's definitely not a 'men only' issue. But it is an area of life with which the majority of men may identify.

Teaching This affects children and adults alike. In most churches the majority of those leading the work with children and young people are female. Of course this may simply reflect the ratio of men to women in the congregation, but more often it reflects a deeper issue. There's an assumption in many churches that children's work is exclusively women's work. This attitude demeans both children and women. Boys need good male role models – now more than ever when so many are brought up in homes where there is no adult male. Youth and children's work should be promoted as one of the crucially important forms of service in the life of the local church. We should be encouraging men who have the appropriate skills and attitudes to play their part in these groups.

The teaching directed at the adult congregation should take account of issues that men face. So anyone with responsibility in this area should check that his or her material uses illustrations and examples that will be relevant for men. The caricatures of men listed in Chapter 2 (page 11) may be used as ways into communicating with men.

Fellowship The sharing of 'the peace' in the Communion Service can be an activity that many men struggle with, particularly if it is accompanied by hugging and kissing. (My friend John said: 'I sit unobtrusively and plan my golf fixtures when we have the peace.')

In many churches coffee is served after the service. Bob said: 'I feel as if I'm supposed to talk to people. If I don't,

Telling stories...

The congregation at Holy Trinity, Brussels, invites visitors to stay on for coffee or to have a drink at the bar after the service. One visitor commented that it was noticeable that the men were far more voluble at the post-service refreshments than in his home church, and that the congregation reflected a much closer balance in the number of men and women attending.

I'm regarded as the odd one out. Yet when I go to the pub I can sit quietly with my drink and not be thought of as odd'. The tension here is that many men feel lonely and long for some deeper interaction with other men, but don't necessarily find the after-church coffee scene very helpful. How can we encourage interaction between men that will put them at their ease and build meaningful relationships?

Leadership There is a tricky issue centred around leadership. In my experience, work amongst men flourishes where there is a male leader who relates well to men. This doesn't have to be a clergyman, but any such work will need the backing of the church leadership team.

The ongoing life of the church

Of course, the life of the local church isn't restricted to Sundays. It's vitally important to integrate men into the whole spectrum of church life without church becoming yet another pressure in already pressurized lives. All too often in the church the gifts and abilities of men are either under-recognized or under-used. It seems as if men are expected to leave behind many of their skills when they become involved in the life of the church.

I've frequently had the depressing experience of sitting through badly-chaired church meetings, while knowing that in the room are people who regularly chair high-powered committees in business or industry. Their companies have spent large amounts of money training them to do so. I'm not recommending that such people are automatically appointed to chair all church meetings. But wouldn't it make sense to 'tap into' their skills on a consultative or training basis? Similarly, a church fabric committee may be struggling with a project: they've searched Yellow Pages for appropriate help, while ignoring the services of a skilled carpenter in the congregation.

The focus of ministry

Making sure that men are fully involved in the day-to-day, week-by-week life of the church is vitally important. It's a crucial aspect of how we 'do church'. But I'm equally convinced that we need to be looking beyond activity, to ask questions that go to the heart of how we *are* as church.

In his book *Being Human, Being Church*, Robert Warren (the Church of England's National Officer for Evangelism) discusses his concern at the inward-looking nature of many aspects of contemporary church life. Few, in his opinion, have adopted what he calls a 'whole-life focus'. Unless we're prepared to ask that kind of question, much of our activity will be the church-life equivalent of re-arranging the deck chairs on the Titanic.

As far as men are concerned, our current situation is a direct consequence of our short-sighted church-life focus. It leads to men feeling mystified by the discrepancy between their experience of 'ordinary' daily life and what happens in church on Sundays. It leads to the false

distinction between work and church. Some men drop out of church because they cannot see its relevance. Others get so caught up in it that their whole life revolves around church; being appointed elder or church warden becomes the height of spiritual achievement.

For the majority of people their ordinary daily life *is* the life to which God has called them. The church should be helping people get excited about the ordinary, about what they do Monday to Saturday, as well as what they do on Sunday. This is the change of attitude that's central to the shift to a whole-life focus.

Unless it's prepared to make this fundamental change, I cannot see the church making much impact on today's men. But if it is, I think men will start to find a church which is ready to help them make sense of life. Such a church will help them to become like Christ. It will help them to encourage others to join them on the journey of Christian faith. This kind of church will not only incorporate men, but inspire them to live lives that make a difference in the world.

Jesus' simple invitation was, 'Come'. He welcomed all people to himself. One of his last words to his followers was 'Go' (Matthew 28:18-20). Jesus longs for men to be part of his transforming purpose for the world. He wants them to make a difference at work, in the family, in the local community; to stand against injustice, racism, poverty, oppression wherever it may be found; to stand for truth, peace, integrity, honour and right living.

The church should reflect the one who is at its head, Jesus. Our invitation should be like his: 'Come' and find a place to encounter Jesus in a way which is relevant and appropriate for you. We should also be able to say: 'Go' from here to make a difference and to be different. We need churches like that – for society's sake, for men's sake, for Christ's sake.

Telling stories...

The Stable is a community-based church in north London. Members keep an urn of coffee simmering in the corner of their meeting room throughout the service. The church leader comments: 'We find this helps men who are used to being able to grab a cup of coffee at work whenever they want to. One policeman regularly comes to church directly from an all-night shift. He tells me that what keeps him coming is knowing that there's coffee waiting to keep him awake.'

Even Mr Right gets it wrong

Women say they want New Man – but, argues Jane Gordon (Daily Telegraph, July 1996), it's the old type who excites.

This week a survey and a book have claimed to reveal exactly what women want. The survey, Visions and Values, set up by the Women's Communication Centre drew its conclusions from 10,000 women who filled in cards - left in shops and slipped into magazines - that asked the seemingly simple question 'What do you want?' The book, *What Women Want* (Virago, £6.99), contains a selection of the 46,000 suggestions put by the respondents...

[I]n no area are the apparent desires of contemporary women more unrealistic than in that of their relationships with men. Women, according to the survey, put a high priority on a 'mutually rewarding relationship' in which they are recognized as being as strong as men. They want thoughtfulness, respect and a 'good man' who treats them well, shows his emotions, is an expert lover and appreciates a woman 'in charge of her own sexuality'. And, of course, they want 'unconditional love' from this paragon. Their description of the ideal man struck a particular chord with me, because coincidentally, the findings of my own, rather less extensive, research into what women want are also published this week. And the difference between the conclusions in my novel *Stepford Husbands* and in *What Women Want* are dramatic.

Last spring and summer, I hosted a series of lunches and suppers for a number of my women friends and acquaintances (my sample group was closer to 100 than 10,000) during which I posed a similar question to that asked by the Values and Visions survey. 'What,' I asked my not entirely random sampling of women, 'do you want from men?' My respondents were, I admit, drawn from a tighter social grouping than that of this new survey. But although they were generally middle class and aged between thirty and forty-five, they were living disparate lives. Some were happily single, others involved in traditional and ostensibly good marriages. A few were in unsatisfactory live-in relationships, others in marriages they found restricting; some were divorced and many were still searching for their version of Mr Right. Almost all of them thought they knew what they wanted: someone who would be caring, who would share the domestic responsibilities and who would be affectionate, attentive and understanding. They said they wanted a man who was 'in touch' - with his emotions, could communicate how he felt and would put home and family before career.

'What I want,' said a friend who has never married, 'is a man who is more like a woman.' Her answer was loudly

supported by the ten other women present on that occasion. Yet I later discovered that those women among my research subjects who seemed closest to having achieved this ideal were as discontented as those who were living with more traditional, chauvinistic men. One, whose husband was looking after the children while she worked full time, said she found him dull, petty, irritating and physically unattractive. 'When I came home from work the other day, he... went on for half an hour about some washing powder he had discovered that prevents woollens from bobbling,' she said.

Another complained that her husband had somehow invaded her traditional territory. She resented his presence in the kitchen, she said, in 'rather the way that so many men still resent women's invasion of what they regard as their territory - the workplace'. She believed that women were nearly as guilty as men of maintaining and encouraging the divide between the sexes.

Indeed, we might think that we would like to turn the brutish British male into a sweet and submissive soul mate, but in reality we do not find 'feminine' traits in men attractive. We might complain about their obsessions with sex and sport, but we would be repulsed if they took a sudden interest in flower arranging or *petit point*.

In fact, after many weeks of exhaustive discussion with my friends, I concluded that what women say they want and what they really want are very different notions. The men we find most attractive, the ones who really excite us, are those who display the most overtly masculine characteristics, not those who do all the ironing, washing up, change the nappies and want to talk endlessly about their innermost feelings.

It is a sad truth that one of the reasons men continue to behave badly is that many women - whatever they might say to the contrary - seem to like it. One or two of us might yearn for the Stepford Husband described by the survey. But most of us remain as confused about what we really want as ever we were.

Somewhere between the traditional ideal of the man as dominant provider and the new vision of the domesticated and emasculated New Man lies a compromise that might result in a partnership - one that not just women but also men might want.

Ideas for changing church

- **Help is at hand** Take a look at the comments made by outsiders concerning your Sunday services (see START HERE on page 8). What changes can you make immediately? What changes require longer term planning? How will you go about these?

- **Radical rethink** Get hold of a copy of *Launching a Missionary Congregation* by Robert Warren (CPAS) and study it as a leadership group, or through your home group system. Identify ways in which you can begin to refocus the life of the church.

- **Up front** Review the impression given by those who are involved 'up front' on Sundays. Is there a balance of men and women, young and old?

- **Him book** Don't choose hymns and songs that use language that's off-putting to men, and that are set at an inappropriate pitch. Check the illustrations and stories used in talks and sermons: how many of them refer to the world of men?

- **Only models need apply** Set an example by making reaching men a priority. If you are a male church leader, identify an activity outside your work life where you can engage with men who aren't Christians. You may want to consider one of the following:

  - Join a gym or health club.
  - Enrol in an evening class.
  - Join a walking/ climbing /cycling group.
  - Learn to scuba dive.
  - Join a local history group.
  - Start (or join) a pub quiz team.
  - Join a local conservation group.

Jesus meets... Peter
Read John 21:1-19

On your marks...

'Do you love me?' It is significant that Jesus asks Simon Peter the question three times. Peter had denied him three times. Here he is given the opportunity to affirm his commitment to Jesus.

Activity You will need two large pieces of paper. Draw a line down the middle of one of them. In one column list all the church activities with which men in your group are involved; in the other column list all the work skills that the men in your group could offer to the life of the church. On the other sheet list the ways in which the church could help the men in the group with their everyday lives as Christians. Remember to be sensitive to any in the group who may not be in full-time paid employment.

Discuss:

• Are there ways men's skills could be better used in the life of the church?
• How could the church better resource men to be Christian in their everyday lives?

Get set...

Jesus meets his disciples after a fruitless night fishing and issues instructions to fish on the other side of the boat (21:5,6).
• What connections can be made between Jesus and our work lives?
• In what ways can we help men to encounter Jesus at their point of expertise?

Jesus prepares a fire of burning coals, together with some fish and bread. He doesn't need their huge catch, but still invites them to bring some of it along (21:9,10), and join him for breakfast (21:12).
• How can we welcome and maximize the wide range of men's skills and abilities?
• What can we do to help men feel relaxed and 'at home' in church?

Jesus reinstates Peter through his threefold questioning (21:15-17).
• How do we handle failure and forgiveness as a church?

• What are the best ways to call men to complete commitment to Christ?

Go!

Man to man Introduce the four characters below. If possible, split into groups, allocating one character per group. Discuss what would help each of these men to come to a living faith.

> *Len* (58) Unemployed for five years; adult children; wife works; minimal contact with church in past; occasionally prays for help.

> *Mark* (36) Upwardly mobile; runs own software company; lives with partner; no children; Christianity seems irrelevant to his successful lifestyle.

> *Mike* (24) Newly released from first prison sentence; few prospects of legal employment; lives with parents at home. Prison chapel is his sole experience of church.

> *Rob* (45) Self-employed builder; recently divorced; enjoys a pint with his mates; works out at gym; has had numerous relationships but finds it hard to settle with anyone; was married in church, but hasn't been back since.

Pray about your activities both inside and outside the church. Pray for your contact men in the light of your discussion of the four men above.

CHAPTER 7

ULTIMATE MENTOR

Jesus: commonly on the lips of men as an expletive, often dismissed as irrelevant. Yet despite the wide gap of culture and time that separates our experience of everyday life from his, Jesus remains the perfect 'mentor' for men today.

A man who served

Jesus didn't need to play power games with people to exert his rights or superiority. Confident in his relationship with his Father, he could lay aside masks, and ultimately lay down his life for others. He calls his followers to copy his example of servanthood (Mark 10:41-45). Many men find such teaching uncomfortable, even threatening. It runs against our society's prevailing view of masculinity. Yet being a servant doesn't mean becoming a doormat. Jesus was far from that. It is a conscious decision to put others' needs before our own. This decision is one that takes great courage. Jesus led from the front. He never expected others to do what he was not prepared to do himself. He took his outer clothes off to wash his disciples' feet, and then invited them to do as he had done (John 13:15).

A man of love

Jesus demonstrated 'tough love' in his daily dealings with people, the kind of love that forgives when your best friend lets you down (John 21:15-19), not once but seventy times seven. It's the kind of love that accepts the weaknesses of those around you rather than condemning them for what they can't be. Such love challenges those who are doing wrong when they should know better. This is no soft, sentimental love, this is the tough love of God. This is the love men need to express.

A man of integrity

Jesus could be relied upon. He lived out what he taught. He spoke of healing the sick and caring for the poor and did just that (Luke 8:26-39). He didn't shy away from people who were unacceptable or conventionally unlovable (Luke 18:35-43). He welcomed them, touched them, and helped them. Jesus could be trusted. He expects the same of his followers. Of course we are going

to get it wrong. Yet we return to him confident of his forgiveness and the power of his Spirit to change us.

A man of truth

Jesus placed great value by truth. A constant refrain of his teaching is 'I tell you the truth...' (See, for example, John 3:3; 5:19; 6:32; 8:34). He told the truth whether it made him popular or not. Today it is almost accepted that we will twist the truth to our advantage, tell part of the truth, or even simply lie if it helps us. Jesus would have none of that. A man carries little respect if he cannot be relied on to be truthful, even when that means owning up when we are responsible for mistakes.

A man with a purpose

Jesus knew what he was meant to do: he was to live in obedience to his Father's will (John 5:19). This would take him to a fear-filled night of prayer. It would lead him to a bloody cross. He didn't allow other people to sway him from doing what God wanted him to do, even those who were close to him. He didn't allow other things to sway him either – the adulation of the crowd, the temptations of the devil, the attraction of power, the opportunity for an 'easy' life. Jesus warns his followers not to 'work for food that spoils but for that which endures to eternal life' (John 6:27). In response, his closest friends asked him, 'What must we do to do the works that God requires?' (John 6:28). He responds, 'The work of God is this, believe in the one he has sent.' Discovery of purpose is to be found through belief in God, the one who made us and gives purpose to life and living. Again men may struggle at this point. The stereotype says we must succeed by ourselves. God says, without me you cannot discover what life is really about.

A man of intimacy

Jesus was not a stranger to intimate relationships. He allowed a woman to wash his feet and dry them with her hair. John's Gospel tells us that he loved her and her sister and brother (John 1:5). Lazarus' sisters called for Jesus' help with the words, 'The one you love is sick' (John 11:3). Learning of his friend's death, he wept (John 11:35,36). When a rich young man declared his faithfulness to the commandments, we are told 'Jesus looked at him and loved him.' (Mark 10:21). One of the disciples is referred to as the 'disciple whom Jesus loved' (John 13:23). He wept over the city of Jerusalem (Mark 8:34-38).

Jesus was in touch with his feelings, a truly passionate man. So many men today are not. A friend of mine recently told me how, despite the fact that he'd been married for eight years, he had decided that he didn't have any feelings. Fortunately after attending a course exploring intimacy in relationships, he was able to confess: 'I am just beginning to realize that I may have emotions after all.' Jesus wants passionate men, who feel deeply and care strongly. This is a challenge to both the 'strong and silent' model of masculinity – and to the traditional British stiff upper lip.

A man of fun

Jesus was not dull: the Gospels give occasional glimpses into his humour. It was his declared intention to bring life in all its fullness (John 10:10). A Christian man is not meant to be stuffy and boring. He is meant to be fully alive, enjoying what God has given in a way which honours the God who gives.

Journey to Christ-likeness

Tony was an unapologetic 'macho man' before his conversion as a young adult. In the subsequent twenty years God has made some huge changes in his life. Today he exhibits a real Christ-likeness in his willingness to serve others. He's no doormat, but he is a *doorman*, an active servant denying his own preferences for the sake of others. He is a man of great strength, willing to stand up against what is wrong, and yet has real tenderness as he feels the pain of those around him. His conversion has affected the way he treats his wife, brings up his children, acts around the home, goes about his work. He has moved beyond a stereotypical idea of masculinity to being more Christ-like, yet he has not lost his original identity as a working-class man. He hasn't simply transferred the mask of macho man for the mask of 'Mr Christian Nice Man'.

Being changed by Jesus is not comfortable, but it is liberating. Being changed by Jesus is not instantaneous, but it is real. Being changed by Jesus is not predictable, but it is exciting. Jesus longs to start from where a man is and help him become man alive – fully alive.

I have been in the privileged position of seeing many different types of men respond to Jesus, men from all walks of life, from very different backgrounds and experiences. I am convinced that Jesus is as relevant today as he ever was, and able to transform the life of any man alive. As part of the process he longs to use our churches and their work among men. What a privilege – and what a challenge!

Ideas for ongoing activity

- **Vision - what would God like to see happen?** If you have issued a prayer leaflet, sift through any responses. Try to gain a sense of what God's agenda is for your church's work among men. As a sense of God's vision develops, try to write it down in a sentence or two. A vision should be forward-looking and try to capture the essence of what you want to see happen. For example: *Our vision is to see all men discover what it means to be a man through the God-man Jesus.* If you can then summarize it in a pithy and memorable phrase, so much the better.

- **Objectives: how are we going to fulfil our aims?** For aims to become reality it helps to have some practical objectives to work to. Take each aim and identify the steps that will need to be taken for it to be fulfilled.

- **Everyman** Review your aims in the light of the comments in Chapter 5. Try to 'think network' as well as 'thinking neighbourhood', to 'think strategically' as well as 'thinking specifically', to 'think process' as well as 'thinking result'. In what ways could your aims be influenced by these considerations?

- **Leadership** 'The single most significant factor in the "success" of a group is a clear, motivated and concerned leader.' Who are going to be your leaders? When they have been identified, don't just appoint those who are responsible for implementing the strategy, make sure that you resource them as well.

  Use the 'triangle of delegation' to ensure that people are enabled to fulfil the task given to them as effectively as possible.

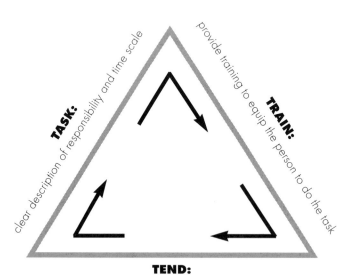

TASK: clear description of responsibility and time scale

TRAIN: provide training to equip the person to do the task

TEND: ensure they are cared for in the process, don't abandon them

- **Men's own** Produce a simple leaflet for the congregation so that anyone who wants to know about the church's strategy for work among men can find out exactly what is going on. Be sure to communicate your strategy in every way possible to those who need to know about it. Doing so once on paper won't be enough. Ultimately, the key principle for helping those who aren't Christians to become Christians is also true for communicating within the church – one to one is best!

Jesus meets... Thomas
Read John 20:24-31

On your marks...

Thomas (20:24) Despite courageously stating he was willing to accompany Jesus and die with him (John 11:16), Thomas is mainly remembered for his doubting nature. But it seems to me that his doubts are perfectly well founded here. He knew that dead people don't come back. I don't think he was any more sceptical than I would have been.

'Unless I see...' (20:25). Note that these are the words of a sceptic not a cynic. The sceptic is open to change, 'Unless I see....' The cynic's mind is closed despite any evidence, 'Even if I see....'

Activity Can you identify some common difficulties that prevent people from accepting the Christian faith: for example, 'Science and Christianity disagree'. List them under the headings HEAD, HEART and WILL.

Discuss:
- How would you respond to some of these issues?
- What do you do if the person you're talking to is a cynic – 'closed' regardless of evidence?

Get set...

Jesus revealed himself in the most unusual way, despite a locked door (20:26). When Thomas eventually met the risen Jesus, he called him 'My Lord, and my God' (20:28).
- To what extent do you think it is our responsibility to reveal Jesus to our contact men? To what extent should we simply leave it to Jesus himself?
- What does it mean to call Jesus 'My Lord and my God?' Do you think men may struggle with any aspects of that statement?

John tells us that Jesus came to give us life in his name (20:31).
- What does life 'in his name' mean for you?
- What does life in his name mean for men today? Is it any different from what it means for women?
- As we think about ways to speak to men about Jesus, what can we learn from Jesus' first words to Thomas on this occasion (20:26)?

Go!

Man to man Discuss your reactions to these seven sessions.

- How will they make a practical difference to your relationships with other people in general, as well as with your contact man?
- Are there practical suggestions you can make to your church leadership team regarding ways to improve the church's strategy for helping men respond to Jesus?
- Are there particular ways in which you would like to pray about men? Could you include them on the prayer list of your home groups? Could prayer for your contact men continue beyond these studies?

Pray Celebrate the life of the group through an act of worship expressing thanks to God for all you have shared. Continue to pray for your contact men.

GOING FURTHER

The following six group sessions offer a structure to help people who wish to 'dig deep' into issues of maleness and masculinity. They provide an opportunity for Christian men to make an honest appraisal of the challenge of change.

Getting started

Leaders will need to feel comfortable discussing personal issues and know how to handle pastoral situations as they arise. They will also need some knowledge of group dynamics so that they can work out the best way to encourage maximum participation. How you run your group will vary according to the cross-section of men within it. Consider the following points:

- *All-age friendly* Older men may find these activities more threatening than younger men. It's important that such men feel safe and valued within the group.
- *Don't patronize* Some groups will include men who aren't Christians. While they need to know that the group will explore masculinity from a Christian perspective, they should also be certain that their opinions will be taken seriously.
- *Be flexible* Some men enjoy practical group activities and find them helpful. Others prefer straight discussion. All of the activities are planned to work with or without the accompanying practical suggestions.
- *Ground rules* A group contract or covenant should be established. This is a mutually agreed way of operating, particularly with regard to attendance and confidentiality. You will need to come to a shared definition of what you mean by confidentiality. For example, is it acceptable for a group member to talk to his partner (without naming names) about what has been said at a meeting?
- *Preparatory session* Advertise the proposed series of meetings and arrange a preparatory session for all those who are interested in attending. Explain the aims of the group and discuss the group contract. In this way those who agree to sign up will know, and be able to influence, what 'they are in for'. Some, of course, may feel that it's not for them - invite them to support the group meetings by praying.

SESSION 1
Telling our stories

Opening activity

Ensure the venue for your meeting is set up to give a friendly, relaxed atmosphere: make sure it doesn't look like a classroom - or a chapel. Give a pencil and a strip of paper to each person. Ask them to write briefly about an interesting event in their life that they think no one else in the group will know about - the more surprising the better! Place all the papers in a container. Remove them one at a time and read them aloud to the group. Try to guess which event applies to which person.

Main focus

Having found out about an event in the life of each person present, invite each group member to try the following exercise. Work in pairs unless the group has fewer than five members. Encourage the men to listen carefully to what people say and try to build up a picture of the issues that each stage of life has thrown up.

Invite each member to take some time to 'talk through your life'. This may seem daunting to some, so to help people focus encourage them to talk about their life a decade at a time: from birth to ten years of age; from ten to twenty, and so on. As much as possible, encourage men to talk about feelings as well as facts. As they address each decade, the following topics may provide useful prompts:

- home
- school
- family
- work
- responsibilities
- joys
- disappointments
- struggles
- bereavement
- involvement with church

Give each person a maximum of ten minutes and make a rule that no one should interrupt. At the end of that time, the person or persons listening may ask questions.

Next, invite group members to discuss the following questions in pairs before feeding back to the larger group:

- What are some of the best experiences in life so far? Give reasons.
- Think of your own father, grandfathers, (even great-grandfathers). In what ways do you think ideas about being a man, son, husband or father have changed for each generation?
- Who was your 'model' of what it means to be a son, man, husband, father? What qualities did they model?
- Why do men often find it difficult to talk about themselves in this way?

Further activity

Bible exploration Look at I Samuel 16 and identify influences on David's transition from boy to man.

Praying together Invite the group to split into pairs for a short time of silent or spoken prayer. Ask them to identify:

- One aspect of their lives so far for which they would like to thank God.
- One problem (from the present or from the past) with which they need help.
- One other man for whom they would like to pray.

SESSION 2
Telling expectations

Opening activity

Invite the group to make a collection of pictures and advertisements from newspapers, magazines and catalogues portraying a wide range of images of men and masculinity. Alternatively, watch the video *Is There One Standard Life?* It shows images of men taken from films and commercials and is available from the Video Department, London Bible College, Green Lane, Northwood, Middlesex HA6 2UW; Tel: (01923) 826061. An excellent pack of photographic discussion starters is available from Working with Men, The B Team, 320 Commercial Way, London SE15 1QN; Tel: 0171 732 9409.

Main focus

Make copies of the following list of stereotypes (see page 11) and distribute to group members. You may also wish to copy the list onto an OHP acetate or flipchart.

- Real men stand on their own.
- Real men are action men.
- Real men are goal-driven.
- Real men like a challenge.
- Real men are achievement-oriented.
- Real men like to be with other men.
- Real men are sexual predators.
- Real men are heterosexual.

Invite group members to give each statement an 'agreement grading' on a scale of one to five, where one equals 'I agree completely' and five equals 'I disagree totally'. Ask them to consider:

- How much they feel they fulfil any of the stereotypes.
- The extent to which they feel expected to fulfil any of the stereotypes.
- What are the influences which form our expectations of what it means to be a man?
- Are any of the expectations in conflict with one another? How do we handle the tensions this creates?

Further activity

Bible exploration Look at 1 Samuel 17. What does David's encounter with Goliath reveal about his understanding of success and of God?

Praying together Invite group members to identify the major expectations that people have of them at the moment? Pray about these in pairs, asking God for wisdom as to how to respond appropriately to them. Encourage them also to pray about any sense of failure they may be struggling with.

SESSION 3
Telling issues

Opening activity

Copy and enlarge the cartoon images. Fix each one in the middle of a large sheet of paper. Use the descriptions in Chapter 3 (page 19) to brief the group on how the pictures represent four possible reactions to the ways in which society is changing. Brainstorm with the group to discover the strengths and weaknesses of each 'type'. Write them on the sheets so that each cartoon is surrounded with both positive and negative statements. You may want to add additional 'types' representing other contemporary reactions to changes amongst men.

When the four sheets have been filled, display so that everyone can see them. Use the following points to guide your discussion.

Main focus

With which (if any) of the four 'types' do group members identify with most closely? With this in mind, how do you feel about the following areas of contemporary life?

- Changes in the workplace: job insecurity; the increasing number of women in many workplaces; unemployment.
- Changes in the home: caring for children; looking after elderly relatives; sharing domestic tasks; balancing the demands of a two-career partnership.
- Changes in the sexual dynamics: developing awareness of one's own and others' sexuality.

What can we learn from this activity about the best ways of dealing with these and other issues of change?

- If a 'macho man' became a Christian, how might his image change? How might coming to faith affect men from the other three groups?
- Does the church prevent men from drawing on the strengths they bring with them to church from home, work and life experience?
- Does it try to conform them to the image of the church, rather than to the image of Christ?

Further activity

Bible exploration What can we learn from David's relationship with Jonathan as described in 1 Samuel 18? What can we learn from Saul's reaction to David in the same chapter?

Praying together Offer to God the images of how you would like to be as a man. Write a prayer which the members of the group could say together asking for God's help to be like Christ.

men

SESSION 4
Telling relationships

Opening activity

Prepare enough sets of four numbered paper strips for each member of the group. Invite them to spend a few minutes considering each of the following questions. Answers should be written on the appropriately numbered strip, which should then be folded and placed in one of four numbered containers.

Strips 1 and 2 What is the most important woman in your life looking for in you? ('Most important woman' may include employer, mother, wife, girlfriend, daughter or minister.) Please give two answers.

Strip 3 What do you consider the most important aspect of close relationships?

Strip 4 What aspect of close relationships causes you the greatest amount of difficulty?

Main focus

Afterwards read out the answers to each question. Now use the following points to guide your discussion.

Strips 1 and 2 Think of what other people expect of you. Which expectations cause you most difficulty. Can you think of any reasons for this? Are all of these expectations appropriate and acceptable? If not, what should you do about them?

Strip 3 How can you develop those aspects of close relationships that mean most to you? Can you apply this to family, friends and society as a whole?

Strip 4 How do you deal with the things you find most difficult in close relationships? Are there ways to handle them better? What images of women does our society promote? What attitudes towards women should we have? How should we promote such attitudes?

Invite group members to get into pairs. Ask them to identify times where they have experienced intense emotions, for example: anger, hate, love, joy, resentment. (This may not be easy for some men, so don't push too hard.)

Discuss the following questions:

- What caused those feelings? How did you handle them?
- Which of these emotions did your parents express when you were growing up?
- What are the 'acceptable' emotions for men to express?
- What are the emotions that are 'unacceptable' when expressed by men?
- Are there emotions that are acceptable in some contexts, but not in others?
- How can we handle anger creatively?
- How can we express intimacy with those we love?

Further activity

Invite group members to brainstorm to make a list of intense emotions expressed by Jesus. Write them on a flipchart or OHP acetate. Discuss what Jesus' example means for us when we think about the expression of our emotions?

Bible exploration Look at 2 Samuel 11,12. What can we learn from David's experiences with regard to relationships and emotions?

Praying together In pairs pray about issues this session has raised. Ask God to help us be Christ-like in our relationships with other people.

SESSION 5
Telling men

Opening activity

This final session is a little different. Take time to celebrate what you have explored and achieved as a group: have a meal together, or at least arrange some special refreshments. Try to evaluate the sessions so far. In particular, try to pick up any issues that people want to take further. You could do this by asking people to reflect in pairs on what has been the most helpful aspect of the group so far. What has been the most difficult to cope with so far?

Main focus

Take some time to reflect on the following questions:

- What sort of men could make a difference for the better in contemporary society?
- What prevents you from being the man you would like to be? Are there ways of overcoming such obstacles?
- As a group, how can we continue to help one another to develop and grow as men?
- Are there ways we could encourage other men to reflect on their understanding of masculinity and grow through the experience?

If you think it appropriate, ask each group member to write his name on a sheet of paper. Now pass the papers on to another group member, who should then write on it something about the paper's owner's contribution to the group that he values, admires or appreciates. When the activity is complete, return the papers to their starting point. Their owners may then take them home to read at their leisure.

Further activity

Worship together Borrow or make a large wooden cross. Place it beside the images you have used in earlier sessions. Distribute Post-it notes to group members. Invite them to think of as many words as possible that describe Jesus' masculinity. If they are able to link these with actual examples from the Gospels of Jesus' words and actions, so much the better. Ask them to write each word (or phrase) on a Post-it, which can then be fixed to the cross.

You may like to do this while listening to some appropriate music and then invite people to say short prayers of gratitude for what Jesus means to them.

Discuss:

- What do you think about the words that have been placed on the cross? Are there any that people feel uncomfortable with? If so, why?
- Do you want to go on praying for one another? How might this be arranged?

Booklist

Men, Derek Cook, *Marshall Pickering*

Men's Groups, Roy McCloughry & Roger Murphy, *Grove Booklets*

The 60 Minute Father, Rob Parsons, *Hodder & Stoughton*

Finding a Voice: Men, women and the community of the church, Mark Pryce, SCM

Organizations

Christian Viewpoint for Men
PO Box 26
SEVENOAKS
Kent
TN15 0ZP
Tel: (01732) 834297

CVM provides practical support and encouragement for evangelism amongst men.

Maranatha Ministries
Belah Place
Barras
Kirkby Stephen
Cumbria
CA17 4ES
Tel: (01768) 341732

Maranatha Ministries run seminars on issues facing men today, as well as producing resources for work with men.